Productivity & Wellness

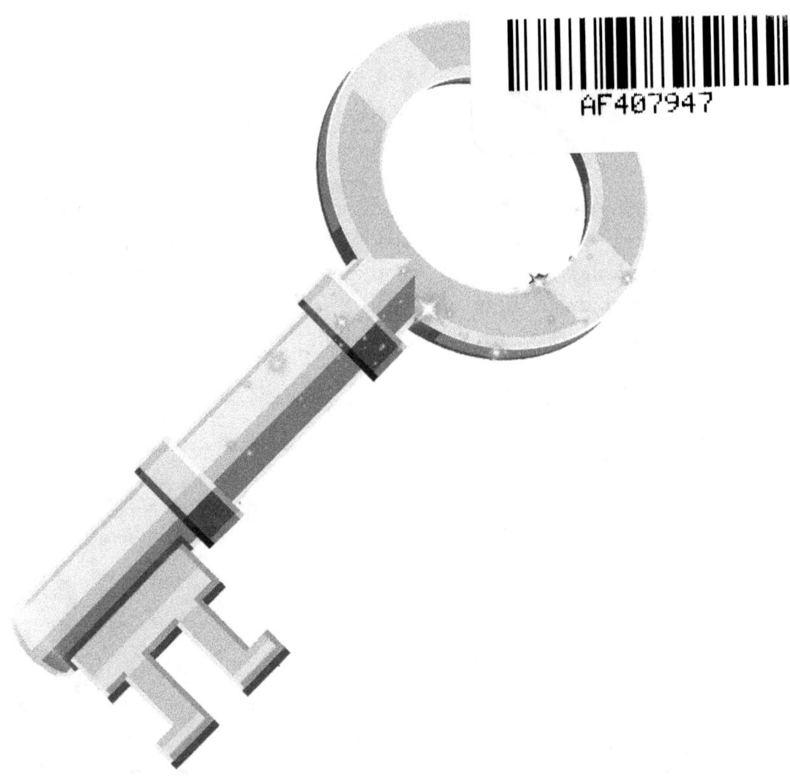

The Key to A Brighter Future

Richard Sharratt

Book design: Russel Davis, Gray Dog Press

ISBN: 979-8-218-35895-2

Printed in the United States of America

Foreword

In the fast-paced, demanding landscape of our modern world, the pursuit of happiness and mental health can sometimes feel like an elusive quest. We often find ourselves caught in a never-ending cycle of tasks, responsibilities, and commitments, struggling to strike a balance between our personal and professional lives. The constant juggling act can take a toll on our mental health, leaving us feeling overwhelmed and disconnected from the very essence of what it means to be human.

Amid this chaos, a beacon of hope shines brightly: productivity. "*Productivity and Wellness: The Key to A Brighter Future*" is a book that explores the profound relationship between productivity and our mental and emotional wellness. It's a journey into the heart of how the way we work and live can significantly impact our lives. In the pages that follow, we'll embark on a captivating exploration of how the principles of productivity, when applied with intention, can become a transformative force in our lives. This book is your guide to unlocking your full potential, finding peace in the midst of chaos, and discovering the key to a more balanced, fulfilling existence.

Through the lens of science, psychology, and real-life experiences, we will delve into the depths of how productivity can reduce stress and anxiety, increase self-esteem, and ultimately pave the way for a happier, more meaningful life. You will discover that productivity isn't merely about doing more; it's about doing the right things, in the right way, with purpose and mindfulness. So, whether you're a student seeking academic excellence, a professional striving for career success, a parent balancing the demands of family and work, or simply someone looking to improve your life, "*Productivity and Wellness: The Key to A Brighter Future*" offers valuable insights, actionable strategies, and inspirational stories to guide you on your quest for improved mental health and overall wellness.

So…get ready to embark on a journey that will empower you to reclaim control over your life, reduce stress, and find a deeper sense of fulfilment. The path to productivity is the path to mental health, and together, we will discover the transformative potential that lies within each and every one of us.

Contents

Chapter 1

The Link Between Productivity and Wellness

In this chapter, we will establish the connection between productivity and mental health. We'll explore the science behind this link, understanding how productivity can reduce stress and anxiety while increasing self-esteem and overall happiness. My real-life examples and little life-hacks that changed my life, through productivity, will be included.

The link between productivity and wellness is not just a matter of perception; it has a strong scientific basis. Research in psychology and related fields has shown how productivity can reduce stress and anxiety while increasing self-esteem and overall happiness. Here's an exploration of the science behind this connection:

Stress and Anxiety Reduction:

The term 'stress reduction' refers to the process or techniques employed to lower or alleviate the physical, emotional, and psychological responses to stress, which can result from various factors such as work pressures, personal issues, or challenging situations. Reducing stress is essential for maintaining mental and physical wellness. Whereas anxiety reduction refers to the process of managing, alleviating, or diminishing the symptoms and impact of anxiety on an individual's mental, emotional, and physical wellness. Anxiety can manifest in various forms, including generalized anxiety, social anxiety, or specific phobias, and it often leads to excessive worry, fear, or nervousness.

Reducing anxiety is crucial for promoting a sense of calm, psychological wellness, and a higher quality of life.

Being productive often involves setting clear goals and priorities. This clarity can reduce the anxiety associated with uncertainty and indecision. Various studies have found that individuals who set specific, achievable goals experienced reduced anxiety levels. Being productive often requires focused attention on tasks, which can be a form of mindfulness. Mindfulness practices have been linked to anxiety reduction. Research published in *Clinical Psychology Review* (2011) has shown that mindfulness-based interventions are effective in reducing anxiety and improving overall psychological wellness.

Here are some examples of what anxiety reduction entails (the science bit):

—Cortisol Regulation:

Stress triggers the release of cortisol, a hormone associated with the body's fight-or-flight response. Chronic stress, where cortisol levels remain elevated, can have detrimental effects on physical and mental health. Productivity often involves effective time management and goal achievement, reducing the pressure and time constraints that lead to stress. A study published in the journal '*Psychosomatic Medicine*' (2023) found that people who perceived themselves as more productive had lower cortisol levels, indicating reduced stress.

—Psychological Control:

Productivity gives individuals a sense of control over their environment and tasks. This perception of control can be a powerful buffer against stress. A recent study revealed that individuals who felt in control of their work-related tasks reported lower levels of stress and higher overall wellness.

Self-Esteem and over-all Happiness encompasses:

—Sense of Accomplishment:

Productivity involves setting objectives, working toward them, and achieving results. The sense of accomplishment that comes from reaching goals can boost self-esteem and self-worth. A study published in the '*Journal of Happiness Studies*' (2023) found a positive correlation between goal attainment and self-esteem.

—Dopamine Release:
Achieving tasks and goals often leads to the release of dopamine, a neurotransmitter associated with pleasure and reward. This release of dopamine can contribute to feelings of happiness and motivation. Studies in '*Nature Reviews Neuroscience*' (2023) have highlighted the role of dopamine in regulating mood and motivation.

The science behind the link between productivity and wellness is rooted in the regulation of stress hormones, the reduction of anxiety through goal setting and mindfulness, and the boost in self-esteem and happiness derived from accomplishments and dopamine release. When individuals engage in productive activities, they often experience a sense of control, clarity, and purpose in their lives, which are essential factors for improving mental health and overall wellness.

It's worth noting that while productivity can be a powerful tool for enhancing mental health, balance is key. Excessive productivity at the expense of rest and relaxation can lead to burnout and adverse effects on mental health. The goal is to strike a healthy balance that promotes wellness and happiness while achieving meaningful goals.

So how do we combat anxiety and stress? Well, there are countless examples of techniques that you can use today to reduce your stress and anxiety, below are just a few:

1. **Deep Breathing:** Taking slow, deep breaths can help relax the body's stress response. For example, when you're feeling overwhelmed before a big presentation at work, taking a few moments to practice deep breathing can calm your nerves and reduce stress.
2. **Physical Exercise:** Regular physical activity, such as jogging, yoga, or swimming, releases endorphins, which are natural mood lifters. Exercise not only reduces stress but also helps maintain overall mental and physical health.
3. **Time Management:** Effective time management techniques can reduce stress by helping individuals prioritize tasks, set realistic goals, and avoid the pressure of last-minute deadlines. For instance,

creating a to-do list and planning your day can help you manage your time more efficiently.

4. **Social Support:** Talking to friends, family, or a therapist can be a powerful stress reduction strategy. Sharing your concerns and seeking advice or empathy can help lighten the emotional burden of stress.

5. **Progressive Muscle Relaxation:** This technique involves tensing and relaxing different muscle groups, which can relieve physical tension and reduce stress. It is often used to manage stress-related conditions like anxiety disorders.

6. **Humour and Laughter:** Laughter triggers the release of endorphins, the body's natural feel-good chemicals. Watching a funny movie or spending time with friends who make you laugh can be an effective way to reduce stress.

7. **Cognitive Behavioural Therapy (CBT):** CBT is a therapeutic approach that helps individuals recognize and reframe negative thought patterns. By changing the way they perceive and respond to stressors, people can reduce the emotional impact of stress.

8. **Aromatherapy:** Some scents, like lavender or chamomile, are believed to have calming effects and can be used in aromatherapy to reduce stress. A few drops of essential oils in a diffuser or bath can provide a soothing experience.

9. **Hobbies and Relaxation Activities:** Engaging in hobbies or relaxation activities that you enjoy, whether it's painting, gardening, or reading, can be a stress-reducing escape from daily pressures.

10. **Healthy Lifestyle Choices:** Eating a balanced diet, getting enough sleep, and limiting the consumption of stimulants like caffeine and alcohol can significantly reduce stress. A well-nourished and rested body is better equipped to handle stress.

11. **Meditation and Mindfulness:** These practices involve focusing on the present moment and calming the mind. Mindfulness meditation, for instance, can be used to reduce stress and increase awareness of thoughts and feelings, helping individuals better cope with stressors.

These examples illustrate the diverse strategies available for reducing stress. The key is to find the techniques that work best for **you** and integrate them into your daily routine to promote a healthier and more balanced life.

Deep Breathing

Deep breathing techniques, also known as diaphragmatic or abdominal breathing, have roots in various ancient practices, including yoga, meditation, and traditional Chinese medicine. These techniques have been used for centuries to promote physical and mental wellness. The concept of deep breathing is central to many relaxation and mindfulness traditions, but it has also gained recognition in modern healthcare for its effectiveness in managing anxiety and stress.

Here's how deep breathing can help someone suffering from anxiety and stress:

1. **Activation of the Relaxation Response:** Deep breathing activates the body's relaxation response, which is the opposite of the "fight-or-flight" response that anxiety triggers. When you breathe deeply and slowly, it signals to your body that you are safe and can help lower your heart rate and blood pressure.

2. **Reduction in Muscle Tension:** Anxiety and stress often cause muscle tension, leading to physical discomfort. Deep breathing helps relax tense muscles, providing a sense of relief and comfort.

3. **Oxygenation of the Body:** Deep breaths ensure that your body receives more oxygen, which is essential for proper functioning. Increased oxygen levels can have a calming effect on the body and mind.

4. **Improved Focus and Mindfulness:** Deep breathing requires concentration on the act of breathing. This focus takes your mind away from the source of stress or anxiety, allowing you to gain better control over your thoughts and emotions.
5. **Reduced Racing Thoughts:** Anxiety often leads to a racing mind with numerous intrusive thoughts. Deep breathing can slow down this thought process, giving you a break from the overwhelming influx of worries.
6. **Enhanced Emotional Regulation:** Deep breathing engages the parasympathetic nervous system, which helps regulate emotions and reduces the impact of the sympathetic nervous system responsible for the stress response.
7. **Lowered Stress Hormone Levels:** Deep breathing can lead to a decrease in the production of stress hormones, such as cortisol. Lowering these hormone levels can result in a reduction of the physical and emotional symptoms of stress.

Here's a step-by-step guide to practicing deep breathing:
1. **Find a Quiet Space:** Choose a quiet and comfortable environment where you can focus without distractions.
2. **Sit or Lie Down:** You can practice deep breathing while sitting or lying down. Ensure you're in a relaxed position.
3. **Breathe in Slowly:** Inhale deeply through your nose, counting to four in your mind as you do so. Feel your diaphragm expand.
4. **Hold Your Breath:** At the top of your inhalation, pause for a moment, counting to two.
5. **Exhale Slowly:** Exhale through your mouth, counting to six in your mind. Feel your diaphragm contract.
6. **Repeat:** Continue this process for several minutes, focusing on your breath and counting as you inhale and exhale.

You can adjust the length of each breath to suit your comfort, but the key is to ensure that your breaths are deep and controlled. Practicing deep breathing regularly, especially during stressful moments, can be a valuable tool for managing anxiety and stress.

Physical Exercise

Physical exercise refers to bodily activities that involve structured movement and exertion of energy. These activities are designed to improve physical fitness, health, or overall wellness. Physical exercise can take various forms, including aerobic exercises, strength training, flexibility exercises, and recreational sports. Engaging in regular physical exercise has numerous benefits for mental health, in addition to its well-documented benefits for physical health.

Here are some examples of physical exercises and how they can improve your mental health:

1. **Aerobic Exercises:** These activities involve rhythmic and continuous movement that increases the heart rate and breathing. Examples include:
   - **Running or Jogging:** Running releases endorphins, which are natural mood lifters. It can reduce symptoms of depression and anxiety.
   - **Cycling:** Cycling can help reduce stress and improve cognitive function. It provides a sense of freedom and relaxation.
   - **Swimming:** Swimming is a full-body workout that can promote relaxation and reduce symptoms of anxiety.
2. **Strength Training:** Strength training involves exercises designed to increase muscle strength and endurance. Examples include:
   - **Weightlifting:** Lifting weights can boost self-esteem, as visible strength gains lead to a sense of accomplishment.

- **Bodyweight Exercises:** Exercises like push-ups and squats can improve body image and confidence as individuals see progress in their physical abilities.

3. **Yoga:** Yoga combines physical postures with mindfulness and deep breathing. It can reduce symptoms of anxiety and improve emotional wellness.

4. **Pilates:** Pilates focuses on core strength, flexibility, and balance. It can enhance body awareness, reduce stress, and improve overall mental health.

5. **Tai Chi:** Tai Chi is a martial art characterized by slow, flowing movements. It can reduce symptoms of depression and anxiety and improve overall wellness.

6. **Dance:** Whether it's formal dance classes or simply dancing to your favourite music, dancing is a fun and effective way to reduce stress, improve mood, and boost self-confidence.

How Physical Exercise improves Mental Health:

1. **Endorphin Release:** Physical exercise triggers the release of endorphins, which are natural mood enhancers. These chemicals help reduce symptoms of depression and anxiety.

2. **Stress Reduction:** Exercise can reduce the production of stress hormones like cortisol. It helps individuals cope with and manage daily stressors more effectively.

3. **Improved Sleep:** Regular physical exercise can lead to better sleep quality, which is essential for mental health. Quality sleep contributes to reduced irritability and mood swings.

4. **Enhanced Self-Esteem:** Achieving fitness goals, feeling stronger, and seeing improvements in one's physical appearance can boost self-esteem and body image.

5. **Cognitive Benefits:** Exercise has cognitive benefits, such as enhanced focus, memory, and problem-solving skills. It can alleviate symptoms of brain-related conditions like dementia.

6. **Social Interaction:** Engaging in group sports or exercise classes can provide opportunities for social interaction, reducing feelings of loneliness and promoting a sense of belonging.

7. **Mind-Body Connection:** Mindful exercises like yoga and Tai Chi promote the mind-body connection, fostering relaxation and emotional balance.

8. **Reduced Symptoms of Mental Health Conditions:** Physical exercise is often used as a complementary therapy for mental health conditions such as depression and anxiety. It can alleviate symptoms and improve overall wellness.

It's important to note that the type and intensity of exercise may vary depending on an individual's physical condition and personal preferences. Engaging in physical exercise as part of a healthy lifestyle can significantly contribute to improved mental health and overall quality of life.

Before taking part in any form of physical fitness, please consult your doctor, if you feel necessary.

Time Management

Time management refers to the process of organizing and prioritizing tasks and activities to make the most effective and efficient use of your time. It involves setting goals, creating schedules, and implementing strategies to ensure that you allocate your time to activities that align with your priorities and objectives. Effective time management is crucial for improving productivity and reducing stress, which, in turn, can have positive effects on mental health. Here are examples of time management strategies and how they can enhance productivity and mental wellness:

Here's some examples of Time Management Strategies:
1. **To-Do Lists:** Creating daily or weekly to-do lists is a simple yet powerful time management technique. It helps you organize tasks and prioritize them based on importance and deadlines.
2. **Prioritization:** Identifying high-priority tasks and focusing on completing them first can prevent the stress associated with last-minute rushes and missed deadlines.
3. **Time Blocking:** Allocating specific time blocks for different tasks or activities helps ensure you have dedicated time for work, relaxation, and personal activities.
4. **Setting SMART Goals:** Using the SMART (Specific, Measurable, Achievable, Relevant, Time-bound) criteria to set clear and realistic goals ensures that your objectives are well-defined and manageable.

5. **Eliminating Distractions:** Identifying and minimizing distractions, such as turning off social media notifications during work hours, can significantly increase productivity and reduce stress.
6. **The Pomodoro Technique:** This technique involves working for a set time (e.g., 25 minutes) followed by a short break. It encourages focused work and regular breaks to prevent burnout.
7. **Batching Tasks:** Grouping similar tasks together and completing them in a single batch can save time and reduce the cognitive load of frequent task-switching.
8. **Time Tracking:** Using time tracking tools or apps to monitor how you spend your time can provide insights into where you can make adjustments for better efficiency.

This is how Time Management enhances Productivity and Mental Health:
1. **Reduces Stress:** Effective time management helps prevent the feeling of being overwhelmed by tasks and deadlines. By planning and organizing your time, you can reduce stress and anxiety.
2. **Improves Focus and Efficiency:** Time management allows you to allocate dedicated periods for focused work, leading to improved productivity. You can complete tasks more efficiently and effectively.
3. **Creates a Sense of Control:** Feeling in control of your time and tasks enhances your self-esteem and self-confidence. This sense of control contributes to positive mental health.
4. **Enhances Work-Life Balance:** Proper time management ensures that you have time for both work and personal life, promoting a healthier balance and reducing burnout.
5. **Boosts Accomplishment:** Crossing tasks off your to-do list and achieving your goals can boost your sense of accomplishment, leading to higher self-esteem and overall wellness.
6. **Prevents Procrastination:** Effective time management strategies can reduce the urge to procrastinate by breaking tasks into manageable steps and setting realistic deadlines.
7. **Better Decision-Making:** When you have a clear sense of your priorities and time commitments, you can make more informed decisions about what to focus on.

Time management is a valuable skill that not only enhances productivity by making the most of your time but also contributes to improved mental health. By reducing stress, enhancing control and efficiency, and promoting a better work-life balance, effective time management can lead to a more fulfilling and healthier life.

Social Support

Social support refers to the assistance, encouragement, and emotional sustenance that individuals receive from their social networks, including friends, family, and peers. This support can take various forms, such as practical help, emotional understanding, or just a listening ear. The concept of social support has its roots in various fields, including sociology, psychology, and medicine. It plays a crucial role in promoting mental health and overall wellness.

Here are some examples of social support and how it can improve your mental health:

1. **Emotional Support:** This involves offering empathy, understanding, and a safe space for someone to express their feelings. For example, when someone is going through a tough time, a friend who listens without judgment provides emotional support.

2. **Practical Support:** This type of support includes tangible assistance, such as helping with household tasks, running errands, or providing transportation. For instance, a family member helping with childcare can reduce the stress of a working parent.

3. **Informational Support:** When someone needs advice, guidance, or information, informational support comes into play. A colleague giving suggestions on how to deal with a challenging project at work is an example of this type of support.

4. **Companionship:** Being there for someone, engaging in shared activities, and spending time together can offer companionship. A group of friends who regularly meet for a hobby like hiking provides companionship and a sense of belonging.
5. **Validation and Encouragement:** Encouragement and validation are forms of support that affirm someone's feelings, decisions, or achievements. When a mentor congratulates a student on their academic achievements, it boosts their self-esteem.
6. **Financial Support:** In times of financial hardship, receiving monetary assistance from friends or family can be a significant form of social support.

How Social Support improves Mental Health:
1. **Emotional Wellness:** Social support helps individuals process and manage their emotions, reducing the risk of depression and anxiety. Sharing thoughts and feelings with someone who understands and empathizes can provide emotional relief.
2. **Stress Reduction:** Having a support system can mitigate the impact of stress. When facing challenging situations, knowing that someone is there to help or provide a listening ear can lessen the emotional burden.
3. **Self-Esteem and Self-Worth:** Supportive relationships can enhance an individual's self-esteem. Feeling valued, validated, and loved by others contributes to a positive self-image.
4. **Coping with Adversity:** Social support aids in coping with life's adversities, such as illness or loss. People are better equipped to face difficult circumstances when they have a network of individuals who can assist and comfort them.
5. **Sense of Belonging:** A sense of belonging is essential for mental health. Being part of a social network and feeling connected to others can combat loneliness and depression.
6. **Resilience:** Social support helps individuals build resilience. Knowing they can rely on others during tough times makes it easier to bounce back from setbacks.

7. **Improved Communication Skills:** Interacting with others within a supportive network can enhance communication skills, leading to better emotional regulation and conflict resolution.

Social support is a vital component of maintaining good mental health. It offers emotional sustenance, reduces stress, and provides a sense of belonging and self-worth. Having a support system can help individuals navigate life's challenges, foster resilience, and ultimately lead to a happier and more balanced life.

Progressive Muscle Relaxation

Progressive muscle relaxation (PMR) is a stress reduction technique that involves systematically tensing and relaxing different muscle groups in the body. It was developed by American physician *Edmund Jacobson* in the early 20th century. PMR is designed to reduce muscle tension, calm the mind, and alleviate physical and psychological stress. The practice involves becoming aware of muscle tension and learning to release it. Here's an explanation of PMR with examples and how it can improve someone's mental health:

How Progressive Muscle Relaxation (PMR) Works:

1. **Awareness:** The practice begins with awareness. You become conscious of the tension in your muscles and identify areas of the body where you feel stress or discomfort.
2. **Tension:** You then deliberately tense specific muscle groups. For example, you might start with your hand and forearm by making a fist and squeezing the muscles as tightly as you can for several seconds.
3. **Release:** After tensing a muscle group, you release the tension suddenly and completely. You pay attention to the sensation of relaxation as the muscles let go.
4. **Mindfulness:** While relaxing the muscles, you focus on the feeling of relaxation. This mindfulness component is essential in PMR.
5. **Progression:** You work your way through the entire body, systematically tensing and relaxing muscle groups from your feet to your head.

How Progressive Muscle Relaxation improves your Mental Health:

1. **Stress Reduction:** PMR is effective in reducing physical and emotional stress. As you release muscle tension, it sends signals to your brain that it's safe to relax, reducing the release of stress hormones like cortisol.
2. **Physical Relaxation:** By learning to release muscle tension, individuals can alleviate physical discomfort and improve their overall sense of wellness.
3. **Anxiety and Panic Management:** PMR is often used as a complementary therapy for anxiety disorders and panic attacks. It helps individuals recognize and manage physical symptoms of anxiety, such as muscle tension and rapid heartbeat.
4. **Improved Sleep:** PMR is helpful for those who struggle with sleep disturbances due to stress or anxiety. Practicing PMR before bedtime can promote relaxation and improve sleep quality.
5. **Coping with Pain:** For people experiencing chronic pain conditions, PMR can provide relief by reducing muscle tension, which often accompanies physical discomfort.
6. **Enhanced Mind-Body Awareness:** By practicing PMR, individuals develop a heightened sense of mind-body awareness, which can lead to better emotional regulation and stress management.
7. **Reduced Symptoms of Depression:** PMR can help alleviate the physical symptoms of depression, such as muscle aches and tension, leading to improved mood.
8. **Enhanced Resilience:** As individuals become more skilled in using PMR, they develop greater resilience to stress and are better equipped to face life's challenges.

It's important to note that PMR requires practice and consistency to maximize its benefits. While it's a simple technique that can be done independently, it's often taught by healthcare professionals or in the context of therapy. With regular practice, PMR can become a valuable tool in promoting your own mental health and overall wellness.

Humour and Laughter

Humour is a complex and multifaceted concept that involves the ability to find things amusing or funny. It encompasses a wide range of expressions, such as jokes, satire, comedy, and wit. Humour can be an effective tool for coping with life's challenges and enhancing mental health. It is a universal human experience that brings joy, light-heartedness, and relief from stress and tension.

Origins and Cultural Significance:

The concept of humour has ancient origins and is found in various forms across cultures. Throughout history, humour has been used in literature, art, and oral traditions to entertain, challenge, and provoke thought. Different cultures have their own styles of humour, including wordplay, slapstick comedy, and satire, which reflect the values and perspectives of those societies.

Examples of Humour:

Humour takes many forms, including:

1. **Jokes and Puns:** Simple jokes, one-liners, and puns are classic forms of humour that rely on wordplay and surprise. For example, "Why don't scientists trust atoms? Because they make up everything."

2. **Satire:** Satirical humour uses irony, sarcasm, or ridicule to critique or mock societal issues, institutions, or individuals. Shows like "The Daily Show" and "Saturday Night Live" use satire to comment on current events.

3. **Comedy:** Stand-up comedians, sitcoms, and comedy films use humour to make people laugh. Comedians like George Carlin or sitcoms like "Friends" are known for their comedic content.
4. **Physical Comedy:** This type of humour relies on exaggerated physical actions and gags to create laughter. Examples include the works of Charlie Chaplin and slapstick comedies.
5. **Absurd and Surreal Humour:** This humour subgenre uses bizarre, illogical, and nonsensical elements to create amusement. Shows like "Monty Python's Flying Circus" are known for this style.

How Humour and Laughter can improve your Mental Health:
1. **Stress Reduction:** Laughter triggers the release of endorphins, which are natural mood enhancers. It can reduce stress and promote a sense of wellness.
2. **Pain Relief:** Laughter has been shown to increase the body's production of natural painkillers, providing relief from physical discomfort.
3. **Social Connection:** Sharing laughter with others fosters social bonds and strengthens relationships. It can reduce feelings of loneliness and isolation.
4. **Enhanced Mood:** Humour and laughter can improve mood and create a more positive outlook on life. They can act as a temporary escape from worries and challenges.
5. **Better Coping Skills:** Humour can provide a coping mechanism in difficult situations. It can help individuals maintain perspective and resilience when facing adversity.
6. **Improved Communication:** Humour can break down barriers and facilitate communication, making interactions more enjoyable and less tense.
7. **Creativity and Problem-Solving:** Humour can stimulate creativity and promote innovative thinking, helping individuals find new solutions to problems.
8. **Enhanced Quality of Life:** Regularly incorporating humour into one's life can lead to an overall improvement in quality of life, with greater satisfaction and wellness.

It's important to note that while humour and laughter can be therapeutic, individual preferences for humour can vary widely. What one person finds funny, another may not. However, integrating humour into one's life, whether through humour therapy, comedy, or other forms of amusement, can be a valuable tool for promoting mental health and enhancing one's overall sense of wellness.

Cognitive Behavioural Therapy (CBT)

Cognitive Behavioural Therapy (CBT) is a widely recognized and evidence-based psychotherapeutic approach designed to help individuals address and manage a variety of mental health issues. It originated in the mid-20th century and is rooted in the work of several prominent psychologists. CBT focuses on identifying and changing negative thought patterns, emotions, and behaviours that contribute to emotional distress and mental health challenges. I personally promote this form of Therapy as I have had to use it within my own life to overcome past events and traumas.

Origins of CBT:

CBT has its roots in the work of psychologists like *Albert Ellis* and *Aaron T. Beck*. In the 1950s, *Albert Ellis* developed Rational Emotive Behaviour Therapy (REBT), emphasizing the role of irrational beliefs in emotional distress. *Aaron T. Beck*, in the 1960s, introduced Cognitive Therapy, focusing on identifying and challenging negative thought patterns. These approaches later converged into what we now recognize as CBT.

How CBT Works: CBT is typically a short-term, goal-oriented therapy that involves structured sessions with a trained therapist. Here's how it generally works:

1. **Assessment:** The therapist and the individual work together to identify specific problems or challenges that the individual is facing. These issues can range from anxiety and depression to phobias, eating disorders, and more.

2. **Identification of Negative Patterns:** Through conversations and various assessment tools, the therapist helps the individual recognize negative thought patterns, emotional responses, and problematic behaviours that contribute to their difficulties.

3. **Challenge and Restructure:** The core of CBT involves challenging and reframing these negative thoughts and beliefs. Individuals learn to identify cognitive distortions (such as all-or-nothing thinking or catastrophizing) and replace them with more balanced and realistic thoughts.

4. **Behavioural Strategies:** CBT often includes behavioural techniques. These might involve exposure therapy (gradual exposure to fears or phobias), relaxation training, or problem-solving skills.

5. **Homework Assignments:** Between sessions, individuals are often assigned homework. This could include practicing new coping strategies, journaling, or using CBT techniques in real-life situations.

Two examples of CBT:

1. **Example 1 – Social Anxiety:** A person with social anxiety might hold the irrational belief that "Everyone is judging me." Through CBT, they learn to challenge this belief, gather evidence for and against it, and develop a more balanced belief like "Some people may notice me, but most are focused on themselves."

2. **Example 2 – Depression:** A person with depression may exhibit cognitive distortions like "cognitive filtering," where they focus only on the negative aspects of situations. In CBT, they learn to recognize this pattern, challenge it, and reframe their thinking to incorporate positive aspects as well.

How CBT Can Improve Mental Health: CBT is a highly effective therapy for improving mental health in various ways:

1. **Positive Thought Patterns:** CBT helps individuals replace negative thought patterns with more positive and realistic ones, reducing symptoms of depression and anxiety.

2. **Behavioural Change:** By addressing problematic behaviours, CBT can help individuals improve their coping skills and reduce the impact of mental health challenges.
3. **Emotion Regulation:** CBT teaches emotion regulation techniques, allowing individuals to manage intense emotions more effectively.
4. **Resilience Building:** CBT enhances problem-solving and coping skills, improving resilience in the face of stressors.

Overall, CBT is an empowering approach that equips individuals with practical tools and strategies to better understand and manage their mental health. It is particularly beneficial for conditions where negative thought patterns play a significant role in symptomatology.

It's important to note that there are many other types of therapies including Neuro-linguistic Programming (NLP) and Eye Movement Desensitization and Reprocessing (EMDR).

Please consult your doctor in order to gain recommendations for which technique would suit your needs best (if required).

Aromatherapy

Aromatherapy is a holistic healing practice that uses the natural aromas of essential oils to promote physical, psychological, and emotional wellness. It involves the inhalation or topical application of these oils to induce relaxation, alleviate stress, and address various physical and mental health concerns. Aromatherapy has ancient origins and has been used in various cultures for centuries.

Origins of Aromatherapy:

Aromatherapy can be traced back to ancient civilizations in Egypt, India, China, and Greece. The use of aromatic plants and their essential oils for healing and wellness was a common practice in these cultures. In ancient Egypt, for example, essential oils were used in religious rituals, medicine, and cosmetics. Over time, aromatherapy evolved and gained recognition in contemporary holistic health practices.

How Aromatherapy Works:

Aromatherapy relies on the use of essential oils extracted from various plant sources. These essential oils are highly concentrated and carry the characteristic fragrance of the plant they are derived from. The aromatic compounds in these oils are believed to have therapeutic properties. Aromatherapy can be administered in several ways:

1. **Inhalation:** Inhaling essential oils through diffusers, steam inhalation, or simply by smelling the oils can have a direct impact on mood and emotions. The olfactory system is closely linked to the limbic system, which plays a key role in regulating emotions.
2. **Topical Application:** Some essential oils are diluted in carrier oils and applied to the skin through massages, baths, or lotions. This method can be used for relaxation and physical wellness.

Examples of Aromatherapy:
1. **Lavender Oil:** Lavender essential oil is often used to induce relaxation, reduce anxiety, and improve sleep. It has a calming and soothing scent.
2. **Peppermint Oil:** Peppermint essential oil is known for its invigorating and refreshing qualities. It can help alleviate mental fatigue and boost focus and concentration.
3. **Eucalyptus Oil:** Eucalyptus oil is often used to clear the sinuses and promote respiratory wellness. Its scent can help reduce congestion and ease breathing.
4. **Chamomile Oil:** Chamomile essential oil is soothing and is commonly used for stress relief and promoting relaxation.
5. **Citrus Oils (e.g., Orange or Lemon):** Citrus oils have uplifting and mood-enhancing properties. They can be used to combat feelings of depression or anxiety.

How using aromatherapy can improve your Mental Health:
1. **Stress Reduction:** Aromatherapy can trigger the release of neurotransmitters that promote relaxation and reduce stress. Inhaling the scents of certain essential oils can have an immediate calming effect.
2. **Mood Enhancement:** Different essential oils have mood-enhancing properties. Aromatherapy can help lift one's spirits, combat symptoms of depression, and promote a positive emotional state.
3. **Improved Sleep:** Many essential oils, such as lavender, are known for their sedative effects. Aromatherapy can improve sleep quality and combat insomnia.

4. **Anxiety Reduction:** Certain essential oils, like chamomile or rose, are believed to reduce anxiety and promote emotional balance.
5. **Mindfulness and Relaxation:** Aromatherapy can be incorporated into relaxation and mindfulness practices, helping individuals achieve a calm and focused state of mind.
6. **Pain Management:** Some essential oils, when applied topically, can reduce pain and discomfort, which can indirectly improve mental health by alleviating distress.

Aromatherapy is a complementary therapy that can be incorporated into your daily routines to promote mental wellness and enhance overall quality of life. It is often used in conjunction with other holistic approaches to mental health and wellness.

Hobbies and Relaxation Activities

Hobbies refer to activities or interests that individuals engage in for leisure and pleasure in their free time. These activities are typically pursued for enjoyment rather than for financial gain or as part of one's profession. Hobbies provide a means of relaxation, creative expression, and personal satisfaction, and they have been a part of human culture for centuries. My hobbies include Photography and Writing, to name a few. I find them to be relaxing whilst also stimulating to the mind.

Origins of Hobbies:

The concept of hobbies has ancient roots. In various historical periods, people have pursued leisure activities, such as music, painting, gardening, or sports, for personal enjoyment. Hobbies have been mentioned in literature and historical records throughout history. The word "hobby" itself has a rich history, with its origins dating back to the 13th century, when it referred to a small, often horse-like toy.

Some examples of Hobbies:
1. **Gardening:** Cultivating plants and tending to a garden can be a therapeutic and creative hobby. It allows individuals to connect with nature and provides a sense of accomplishment.
2. **Playing a Musical Instrument:** Learning to play an instrument, whether it's the piano, guitar, or violin, is a hobby that promotes creativity and offers a way to express emotions.

3. **Painting and Drawing:** Visual arts like painting and drawing allow for creative expression and can serve as a form of stress relief and self-expression.
4. **Reading:** Reading books, magazines, or other written materials is a popular hobby that offers an escape into different worlds, fosters imagination, and provides intellectual stimulation.
5. **Cooking and Baking:** Experimenting with recipes and preparing delicious meals can be both a relaxing and rewarding hobby.
6. **Sports and Physical Activities:** Engaging in sports like swimming, cycling, or hiking, or participating in fitness activities like yoga or Pilates, can improve physical and mental wellness.

How hobbies can improve your Mental Health:
1. **Stress Reduction:** Engaging in hobbies can serve as a form of stress relief, allowing individuals to temporarily escape from the demands and pressures of daily life.
2. **Mood Enhancement:** Hobbies that bring joy and satisfaction can boost one's mood and reduce symptoms of depression or anxiety.
3. **Cognitive Stimulation:** Hobbies that challenge the mind, like puzzles, crosswords, or learning a new language, provide cognitive stimulation and can improve mental sharpness.
4. **Social Interaction:** Many hobbies, such as team sports, clubs, or group activities, offer opportunities for social interaction, reducing feelings of isolation and fostering a sense of belonging.
5. **Sense of Accomplishment:** Progressing in a hobby and achieving personal goals can boost self-esteem and provide a sense of accomplishment.
6. **Mindfulness and Relaxation:** Hobbies that require focus and concentration, like meditation, knitting, or painting, can promote mindfulness and relaxation, reducing anxiety and promoting emotional wellness.
7. **Routine and Structure:** Pursuing hobbies can establish a healthy routine and structure in one's life, which is beneficial for mental health.

8. **Personal Fulfilment:** Hobbies provide an avenue for personal fulfilment and self-expression, allowing individuals to explore their interests and passions.

Hobbies are an integral part of human culture and have been practiced for centuries. They offer numerous benefits for mental health, including stress reduction, mood enhancement, cognitive stimulation, social interaction, and a sense of accomplishment. Encouraging others, as well as yourself, to pursue their hobbies and interests can contribute to your overall wellness and quality of life.

Healthy Lifestyle Choices

Lifestyle choices refers to the conscious decisions and behaviours individuals make in their daily lives that have a significant impact on their overall wellness and quality of life. These choices encompass various aspects of life, including diet, physical activity, sleep, stress management, and social interactions. Lifestyle choices play a crucial role in shaping one's mental and physical health.

The origins of Lifestyle Choices:

The concept of lifestyle choices is deeply intertwined with the history of public health and the study of how personal behaviours and decisions can influence health outcomes. The promotion of healthy lifestyle choices gained prominence in the 20th century with the emergence of epidemiology and a greater understanding of the relationship between lifestyle and health.

Some examples of healthy Lifestyle Choices:

1. **Diet:** Choosing to consume a balanced and nutritious diet that includes fruits, vegetables, whole grains, lean proteins, and limited processed foods is a positive lifestyle choice. Conversely, excessive consumption of sugary, fatty, or processed foods can negatively impact health.

2. **Physical Activity:** Engaging in regular physical activity, such as walking, cycling, or sports, is a healthy lifestyle choice. Leading a sedentary lifestyle with minimal exercise can have adverse effects on physical and mental health.

3. **Sleep:** Prioritizing a consistent sleep schedule and getting an adequate amount of sleep is crucial for mental wellness. In contrast, insufficient or irregular sleep can lead to sleep disorders and negatively impact mood and cognitive function.
4. **Stress Management:** Adopting stress-reduction techniques like mindfulness, meditation, or yoga is a positive lifestyle choice. Failing to manage stress effectively can lead to mental health issues like anxiety and depression.
5. **Social Interaction:** Maintaining social connections and nurturing relationships is an important lifestyle choice. Isolation and loneliness can have detrimental effects on mental health.
6. **Substance Use:** Refraining from the misuse of substances like alcohol, tobacco, and drugs is a vital lifestyle choice. Overindulgence can contribute to addiction, mental health disorders, and physical health problems.

How better Lifestyle Choices can improve your Mental Health:
1. **Emotional Resilience:** Making healthy lifestyle choices can enhance emotional resilience, helping individuals better cope with stress and adversity.
2. **Positive Mood:** Engaging in physical activity and maintaining a balanced diet can release endorphins and improve mood, reducing the risk of mood disorders like depression.
3. **Stress Reduction:** Effective stress management techniques, including mindfulness and relaxation practices, can reduce the impact of stress on mental health.
4. **Cognitive Function:** Adequate sleep and a balanced diet support optimal cognitive function, helping individuals think clearly and make sound decisions.
5. **Enhanced Social Connections:** Prioritizing social interaction and maintaining relationships can reduce feelings of loneliness and isolation, contributing to better mental health.
6. **Prevention of Mental Health Disorders:** Healthy lifestyle choices can help prevent the development of mental health disorders and reduce the risk of relapse in those already experiencing such conditions.

7. **Quality of Life:** Ultimately, lifestyle choices have a profound impact on one's overall quality of life. Engaging in healthy behaviours promotes a sense of wellness and life satisfaction.

Lifestyle choices are personal decisions that significantly affect one's mental health. By making positive choices in areas like diet, physical activity, stress management, social interaction, and substance use, individuals can improve their mental wellness, enhance emotional resilience, and reduce the risk of mental health disorders. These choices are pivotal in achieving a balanced and fulfilling life.

Meditation and Mindfulness

Meditation and mindfulness are practices that promote mental and emotional wellness by encouraging self-awareness, focus, and relaxation. These practices have ancient origins and have been embraced in various cultures and spiritual traditions. They are valuable tools for improving mental health in today's fast-paced and often stressful world.

Meditation:

Meditation is a practice that involves training the mind to achieve a heightened state of awareness and a deep sense of inner calm. Its origins can be traced back to various ancient traditions, including Buddhism, Hinduism, and Taoism. Meditation encompasses a wide range of techniques, but most involve focused attention, controlled breathing, and a quiet environment.

An example of Meditation:

One common form of meditation is **mindfulness meditation**, where individuals focus their attention on their breath and observe their thoughts and sensations without judgment. The goal is to be fully present in the moment. Another form is **transcendental meditation**, where individuals silently repeat a mantra to achieve a state of restful alertness.

Mindfulness:

Mindfulness is a state of non-judgmental awareness of the present moment. It involves being fully engaged in what you're doing, noticing your thoughts and emotions, and accepting them without judgment. While mindfulness is often associated with meditation, it can also be practiced in everyday life.

An example of Mindfulness:

Eating mindfully is a common practice. When you eat mindfully, you pay full attention to the taste, texture, and smell of your food, savouring each bite. This can lead to a greater enjoyment of the meal and an increased awareness of hunger and fullness cues.

How Meditation and Mindfulness can improve your Mental Health:

1. **Stress Reduction:** Both meditation and mindfulness can activate the body's relaxation response, reducing the production of stress hormones. This can alleviate the physical and emotional symptoms of stress and anxiety.

2. **Emotion Regulation:** These practices help individuals develop better emotional regulation skills, enabling them to manage negative emotions and cultivate positive ones.

3. **Improved Focus:** Meditation and mindfulness enhance concentration and attention, which can be particularly helpful for individuals with attention difficulties or anxiety.

4. **Better Sleep:** Regular practice can improve sleep quality and help with insomnia by promoting relaxation and reducing racing thoughts.

5. **Enhanced Self-Awareness:** Both practices encourage self-reflection and self-awareness, helping individuals gain a deeper understanding of their thoughts, emotions, and behaviours.

6. **Reduced Symptoms of Depression:** Meditation and mindfulness have been shown to reduce symptoms of depression by promoting a positive outlook and emotional resilience.

7. **Pain Management:** These practices can help individuals cope with chronic pain and discomfort by changing their perception of pain and increasing pain tolerance.

8. **Enhanced Resilience:** Regular meditation and mindfulness practice can improve resilience, enabling individuals to better handle life's challenges and bounce back from setbacks.

9. **Mind-Body Connection:** Both practices promote a stronger connection between the mind and body, which can lead to better physical and mental health.

How to begin meditating:

1. **Choose a Quiet and Comfortable Space:** Find a quiet and comfortable space where you won't be easily distracted. It could be a corner of a room, a garden, or any place that feels serene.

2. **Set a Time:** Decide on the duration of your meditation session. If you're new to meditation, start with just a few minutes (e.g., 5-10 minutes) and gradually increase the time as you become more comfortable with the practice.

3. **Select a Posture:** You can meditate while sitting in a chair, on a cushion, or even lying down. The key is to maintain an upright posture to stay alert and prevent falling asleep.

4. **Focus on Your Breath:** Close your eyes if you're comfortable doing so. Start by taking a few deep breaths to relax. Then, shift your attention to your breath. Notice the sensation of the breath as it enters and leaves your body. You can focus on the rise and fall of your chest or the feeling of the air passing through your nostrils.

5. **Observe Your Thoughts:** As you focus on your breath, thoughts will naturally arise. This is normal. Instead of pushing thoughts away, observe them without judgment. Imagine your thoughts as clouds passing by in the sky.

6. **Return to the Breath:** When you notice that your mind has wandered and you're lost in thought, gently bring your focus back to your breath. It's important to be patient with yourself; it's okay for the mind to wander, and the practice is in the returning.

7. **Body Scan (Optional):** Some mindfulness meditation practices include a body scan. In this technique, you systematically bring awareness to different parts of your body, noting any tension or sensations.

8. **End Mindfully:** To conclude your meditation, take a few deep breaths, open your eyes, and slowly transition back to your daily activities. It's essential to carry the sense of mindfulness with you as you go about your day.

Remember that mindfulness meditation is a skill that improves with practice. Don't be discouraged by a busy mind or distractions; this is a common experience for meditators of all levels. Over time, you'll likely experience the benefits of reduced stress, increased self-awareness, and improved mental wellness.

Chapter 2

Defining Productivity

To be productive, you first need to understand what it means. We will discuss the difference between "busyness" and true productivity. This chapter will help you identify your goals, priorities, and time-wasters, allowing you to start making positive changes. The concept of productivity has a rich history that has evolved over time. It has been influenced by economic, industrial, and technological changes. Here's a brief overview of its historical development:

1. **Agricultural Productivity:** The concept of productivity dates back to pre-industrial times when productivity was primarily associated with agriculture. It was about getting more output from the same or less input, like increasing crop yields without using more land.

2. **Industrial Revolution:** The Industrial Revolution in the late 18th and 19th centuries marked a significant shift in the concept of productivity. It was characterized by the mechanization of labour, which greatly increased output per worker. Productivity became closely tied to factory and assembly line processes.

3. **Taylorism and Scientific Management:** In the early 20th century, *Frederick W. Taylor* introduced scientific management principles. This approach aimed to optimize work processes and worker

efficiency. Taylor's methods became the foundation for modern productivity techniques and emphasized time and motion studies.

4. **Post-WWII Economic Growth:** In the post-World War II era, productivity became synonymous with economic growth. Increased productivity was seen as a means to improve living standards, and governments and businesses alike focused on enhancing efficiency and output.

5. **Information Age:** With the advent of the Information Age in the late 20th century, productivity expanded beyond physical production to include knowledge, work and information management. Technological advancements, particularly in computing, revolutionized the way people worked.

6. **Contemporary Trends:** Today, the concept of productivity encompasses a wide range of areas, from personal time management to organizational efficiency. The rise of the digital age has led to the development of productivity software and tools that aid individuals and businesses in managing tasks, projects, and communication.

This all being good and well, but what does the term 'Productivity' mean to us in today's world, I hear you asking yourself.

Well, the modern interpretation of productivity encompasses various dimensions:
1. **Efficiency:** Productivity is about achieving more with fewer resources. It's the art of optimizing processes and reducing waste in time, energy, and materials.

2. **Time Management:** Effective time management is a cornerstone of productivity in the modern context. It involves setting priorities, avoiding distractions, and using time efficiently.

3. **Quality and Innovation:** Productivity doesn't mean just doing more; it means doing more of the right things. Quality and innovation are key aspects of modern productivity, ensuring that the output is valuable and competitive.

4. **Technological Integration:** In today's digital age, productivity often involves leveraging technology and software tools for tasks such as project management, communication, and automation.

5. **Work-Life Balance:** Modern productivity recognizes the importance of work-life balance. It's not just about maximizing work output but also ensuring that work doesn't overshadow personal and family life.

6. **Personal Development:** On a personal level, productivity is associated with self-improvement, setting, and achieving personal goals, and maintaining a balanced and fulfilling life.

7. **Sustainability:** Productivity in the 21st century is also increasingly associated with environmental sustainability. It's about finding ways to produce more while reducing negative impacts on the environment.

The modern interpretation of productivity has expanded beyond traditional manufacturing and industrial settings to encompass a broad range of personal, professional, and societal contexts. It's about achieving efficiency, balance, and quality in a rapidly changing world where technology and information play a central role.

Efficiency

Efficiency refers to the ability to achieve a desired outcome with the least number of wasted resources, including time, effort, and materials. It is a concept rooted in the field of economics and industrial engineering but is applicable to various aspects of life, including work, personal tasks, and time management.

Origins of Efficiency:

The concept of efficiency has a long history and can be traced back to the Industrial Revolution in the 18th and 19th centuries, which brought about significant advancements in manufacturing and production processes. Engineers and economists began to study and optimize how resources were used to maximize output while minimizing waste. Over time, efficiency principles spread to various fields, including business, management, and personal productivity.

Examples of Efficiency:

1. **Manufacturing:** In a factory, efficiency might involve optimizing production processes to reduce the time and materials required to create a product. For instance, automating certain tasks can improve efficiency by reducing labour costs and time.

2. **Time Management:** In daily life, efficiency can be applied to time management. For example, using time management techniques like the Pomodoro Technique, which breaks work into focused intervals followed by short breaks, can make work more efficient.

3. **Energy Efficiency:** In the context of energy consumption, making buildings and appliances more energy-efficient can reduce waste and lower utility costs. For instance, using energy-efficient LED bulbs instead of incandescent bulbs saves both energy and money.

4. **Resource Allocation:** In business, efficient allocation of resources can involve distributing a budget or workforce to maximize productivity and profitability. It may mean reallocating staff to areas where they are most needed or investing in projects with the highest return on investment.

How being more efficient can improve your Mental Health:

1. **Reduced Stress:** Efficient time management and work processes can reduce stress by preventing overwhelm and the feeling of being constantly rushed.

2. **Increased Productivity:** When tasks are completed efficiently, individuals often feel a sense of accomplishment and higher productivity. This can boost self-esteem and motivation.

3. **Improved Work-Life Balance:** Efficiency allows for better work-life balance by helping individuals complete tasks more quickly and effectively, leaving more time for relaxation and leisure.

4. **Better Organization:** Being organized is a key aspect of efficiency. An organized environment and routine can reduce mental clutter and increase mental clarity and wellness.

5. **Goal Achievement:** Efficiency is instrumental in setting and achieving goals. Accomplishing goals can provide a sense of purpose and satisfaction, contributing to mental wellness.

6. **Reduction in Procrastination:** Efficient time management can reduce procrastination, which is a common source of stress and anxiety.

7. **Enhanced Focus:** Efficient work processes often lead to better concentration and focus, which can improve mental health by reducing distractions and feelings of being overwhelmed.

8. **Enhanced Problem-Solving:** Efficiency can help individuals think more clearly and approach problems with a structured and organized mindset, which is essential for reducing stress associated with problem-solving.

Efficiency is a valuable concept that, when applied to various aspects of life, can lead to improved mental health. It reduces stress, increases productivity, and helps individuals maintain a better work-life balance, all of which contribute to enhanced wellness.

Becoming more efficient involves making better use of your time, resources, and efforts to achieve your goals with less wasted energy. Here are steps to help you become more efficient:

1. **Set Clear Goals:** Define your short-term and long-term goals. Knowing what you want to achieve will help you prioritize tasks and stay focused on what's most important.
2. **Prioritize Tasks:** Identify the most important tasks and responsibilities. Use techniques like the **Eisenhower Matrix** (quadrant of urgency and importance) to determine what needs immediate attention and what can be delegated or delayed.
3. **Time Management:** Develop strong time management skills. Use techniques like the **Pomodoro Technique** (work in focused intervals with breaks), time blocking (assign specific time slots to tasks), and to-do lists to organize your day effectively.
4. **Organize Your Space:** Maintain an organized work environment. A clutter-free space can reduce distractions and help you find what you need quickly. Implement efficient filing systems for documents and digital files.
5. **Delegate Tasks:** Don't try to do everything yourself. Delegate tasks that others can handle, freeing up your time for more critical responsibilities.
6. **Eliminate Distractions:** Identify and minimize distractions in your work environment. Turn off unnecessary notifications, create a quiet workspace, and set specific times for checking emails and social media.
7. **Batch Similar Tasks:** Group similar tasks together. For example, respond to emails in batches, schedule meetings back-to-back, or handle all your phone calls during a specific time window. This minimizes context switching and maximizes efficiency.

8. **Use Technology Wisely:** Utilize productivity tools and software to streamline tasks. Project management software, task management apps, and calendar applications can help you stay organized and efficient.
9. **Set Deadlines:** Establish clear deadlines for your tasks and projects. Having a sense of urgency can boost motivation and efficiency.
10. **Time-saving Tools and Automation:** Investigate and implement time-saving tools and automation. For example, use email filters and rules to sort incoming emails automatically or use scheduling tools to book appointments without back-and-forth communication.
11. **Continuous Learning:** Continuously seek to improve your skills and knowledge. Learning new techniques, software, or strategies can lead to increased efficiency.
12. **Self-care and Wellness:** Take care of your physical and mental health. Proper nutrition, exercise, and regular breaks are essential for maintaining high productivity and efficiency.
13. **Monitor Progress:** Regularly review your progress and make adjustments as necessary. Analyse your efficiency, identify areas for improvement, and adapt your strategies accordingly.
14. **Time for Reflection:** Dedicate time for reflection and planning. Regularly evaluate your goals and accomplishments to ensure you're on the right path.
15. **Seek Feedback:** Ask for feedback from peers or mentors. They can provide valuable insights and suggestions for improvement.
16. **Celebrate Achievements:** Recognize and celebrate your achievements, no matter how small. This positive reinforcement can motivate you to maintain your efficiency efforts.

Becoming more efficient is an ongoing process that requires self-awareness, planning, and the willingness to make changes. By implementing these steps and continuously refining your approach, you can significantly enhance your efficiency and productivity in both your personal and professional life.

Pomodoro Technique

The Pomodoro Technique is a time management and productivity method developed by *Francesco Cirillo* in the late 1980s. The technique is named after the Italian word for "tomato," inspired by the tomato-shaped kitchen timer that Cirillo initially used to time his work intervals. The Pomodoro Technique is designed to improve efficiency and focus by breaking work into short, focused intervals, usually 25 minutes in duration, followed by a short break.

How the Pomodoro Technique Works:
1. **Choose a Task:** Select the task you want to work on.
2. **Set a Timer:** Set a timer for 25 minutes (one Pomodoro).
3. **Work Intensely:** Work on the chosen task with complete focus and dedication until the timer rings. Avoid all distractions during this time.
4. **Take a Short Break:** When the timer rings, take a 5-minute break to rest, stretch, or do something enjoyable.
5. **Repeat:** After completing a Pomodoro (a 25-minute work interval followed by a 5-minute break), restart the timer and work for another Pomodoro. After four Pomodoros, take a longer break, typically 15-30 minutes.

So, let's say you're working on a report using the Pomodoro Technique:
1. Start a Pomodoro timer for 25 minutes.

2. Work intensively on your report, writing, researching, and organizing information during this time.
3. When the timer rings, stop working immediately, even if you're in the middle of a sentence or task.
4. Take a 5-minute break to walk around, stretch, or relax. You could grab a snack or quickly check your messages, but avoid getting caught up in a lengthy distraction.
5. Begin another Pomodoro for 25 minutes of focused work.
6. After completing four Pomodoros, take a longer break of 15-30 minutes to recharge.

How using the Pomodoro Technique can improve your efficiency:
1. **Time Management:** The Pomodoro Technique helps individuals allocate time effectively to tasks. Knowing that you have a limited timeframe to work can enhance focus and reduce procrastination.
2. **Task Breakdown:** Breaking work into manageable, 25-minute chunks makes tasks appear less daunting. This can reduce feelings of overwhelm and make work more approachable.
3. **Increased Focus:** The short, timed intervals encourage undivided attention to the task at hand. This minimizes multitasking and promotes deep work.
4. **Prevention of Burnout:** The regular breaks prevent burnout by allowing brief periods of rest, which can be vital for maintaining energy and creativity.
5. **Adaptability:** The technique is highly adaptable and can be applied to various tasks and projects. It is particularly useful for tasks that require concentration and creativity.
6. **Time Tracking and Improvement:** Over time, individuals can assess how many Pomodoros specific tasks require. This helps in estimating the time needed for future tasks and improving time management.
7. **Accountability:** The technique creates a sense of accountability and discipline. Knowing you need to complete a Pomodoro can help you resist distractions.

The Pomodoro Technique is a simple and effective way to enhance efficiency and productivity by optimizing work intervals and breaks. It's especially useful for individuals looking to manage their time more effectively and maintain a high level of focus and motivation.

Pomodoro Technique: Practice

The technique uses a timer to break down work into intervals, traditionally 25 minutes in length, separated by short breaks.

EACH POMODORO IS ____ MINUTES LONG AND EACH BREAK IS ____ MINUTES LONG

TASK	POMODORO	DONE!
	○ ○ ○ ○ ○ ○ ○ ○	
	○ ○ ○ ○ ○ ○ ○ ○	
	○ ○ ○ ○ ○ ○ ○ ○	
	○ ○ ○ ○ ○ ○ ○ ○	

Eisenhower Matrix

The Eisenhower Matrix, also known as the Eisenhower Box, is a time management and prioritization tool that helps individuals categorize tasks based on their urgency and importance. It was popularized by *President Dwight D. Eisenhower*, who was known for his ability to manage his time effectively and make crucial decisions. The matrix is a simple and visual way to organize and prioritize tasks, helping individuals improve their efficiency and focus on what truly matters.

How the Eisenhower Matrix Works. The matrix consists of four quadrants:
1. **Urgent and Important (Do First):** Tasks in this quadrant require immediate attention and should be completed as a priority. They have a direct impact on your goals or wellness. Examples might include a pressing deadline, a critical work task, or a medical emergency.
2. **Important, but Not Urgent (Schedule):** Tasks in this quadrant are important for long-term goals or personal development but don't have an immediate deadline. They should be scheduled and worked on regularly. Examples include exercise, long-term projects, and strategic planning.
3. **Urgent, but Not Important (Delegate):** Tasks in this quadrant are often distractions or interruptions that demand immediate attention, but don't contribute significantly to your long-term goals. Whenever possible, delegate or minimize these tasks. Examples

include excessive emails, unimportant phone calls, or low-priority meetings.

4. **Not Urgent and Not Important (Eliminate):** Tasks in this quadrant are neither urgent nor important and can be seen as time-wasters. They should be minimized or eliminated from your to-do list. Examples might include excessive social media scrolling, unproductive meetings, or trivial tasks.

Let's say you're managing your work tasks using the Eisenhower Matrix:

- **Urgent and Important (Do First):** You have a critical project deadline that is due today. This falls into the "Do First" category, and you should work on it immediately.
- **Important, but Not Urgent (Schedule):** You've set a goal to improve your skills in your field. While not immediately pressing, you should allocate regular time on your schedule to attend courses or engage in self-study to achieve this long-term objective.
- **Urgent, but Not Important (Delegate):** You receive a phone call from a colleague asking for minor assistance that doesn't align with your priorities. In this case, consider delegating the task or asking them to contact someone more suitable.
- **Not Urgent and Not Important (Eliminate):** You find that you spend a lot of time responding to non-essential emails or attending meetings that don't contribute to your goals. Consider reducing or eliminating such activities to free up your time for more meaningful tasks.

How using the Eisenhower Matrix can improve your efficiency:

1. **Effective Prioritization:** The matrix helps you focus on tasks that have the most significant impact on your goals, avoiding the trap of busywork.
2. **Time Management:** It encourages you to allocate your time wisely, ensuring that both urgent and important tasks are addressed appropriately.
3. **Stress Reduction:** By categorizing tasks, you can reduce the stress and anxiety associated with last-minute rushes and missed deadlines.

4. **Better Decision-Making:** The matrix assists in making better decisions about what to do, delegate, schedule, or eliminate.
5. **Productivity:** It promotes efficiency by ensuring that your time and energy are invested in tasks that align with your goals.
6. **Work-Life Balance:** By addressing important but not urgent tasks (Quadrant 2), you can maintain a better work-life balance and invest time in personal development and wellness.

The Eisenhower Matrix is a practical tool for enhancing efficiency and productivity by helping you determine where to direct your focus and effort. It is especially valuable for individuals looking to make more intentional decisions about task prioritization and time management.

Time Management

Time management is the practice of planning, organizing, and controlling how one uses their time to achieve specific goals, tasks, or activities efficiently. It involves setting priorities, allocating time to various activities, and minimizing time wasted on unproductive tasks. Effective time management can significantly impact productivity, reduce stress, and contribute to better mental health.

Origins of Time Management:

The concept of time management has ancient roots, but its formal study and development as a field emerged in the 20th century. *Frederick Winslow Taylor,* an American engineer, is often considered the father of scientific management. Taylor's work on industrial efficiency and the division of labour laid the foundation for modern time management principles. Over time, time management has evolved, incorporating various techniques and strategies.

Some examples are:

1. **To-Do Lists:** Creating daily to-do lists is a common time management practice. Prioritize tasks and allocate time slots to tackle specific items on your list. For example, you may allocate the morning for high-priority work tasks and the afternoon for less critical tasks.

2. **Time Blocking:** This technique involves blocking off specific periods in your schedule for different types of tasks. For instance, you might allocate the first two hours of your workday for

focused, deep work and the later part of the day for meetings and administrative tasks.

3. **Pareto Principle (80/20 Rule):** The Pareto Principle suggests that 80% of results come from 20% of efforts. Time management based on this principle involves identifying and focusing on the most critical tasks that yield the most significant results.

4. **Task Prioritization:** Categorize tasks by urgency and importance using techniques like the Eisenhower Matrix. This helps you determine which tasks require immediate attention and which can be scheduled or delegated.

5. **Time Tracking:** Keeping track of how you spend your time can reveal patterns and areas where time is often wasted. Tools like time-tracking apps can help in this regard.

6. **Goal Setting:** Set clear, achievable goals and establish a timeline for their completion. Break long-term goals into smaller, manageable steps with deadlines.

How Time Management can improve your Mental Health:
1. **Stress Reduction:** Effective time management can reduce stress and anxiety by helping individuals meet deadlines and prevent the feeling of being overwhelmed.

2. **Better Work-Life Balance:** By allocating time intentionally to work, personal life, and self-care, time management promotes a healthier work-life balance.

3. **Enhanced Focus:** Prioritizing and structuring tasks can enhance concentration and reduce distractions, leading to better mental clarity and focus.

4. **Increased Productivity:** Proper time management ensures that work is completed efficiently, leading to a sense of accomplishment and improved self-esteem.

5. **Time for Self-Care:** Allocating time for relaxation, hobbies, and self-care activities enhances overall wellness and mental health.

6. **Improved Decision-Making:** Time management encourages individuals to make informed decisions about task prioritization and allocation of resources, which can reduce stress and prevent errors.

7. **Reduced Procrastination:** A well-structured schedule helps reduce procrastination, which is often a source of stress and anxiety.
8. **Sense of Control:** Time management provides a sense of control over one's daily activities, leading to reduced stress and greater satisfaction.

Time management is a valuable practice for enhancing efficiency, productivity, and overall wellness. By implementing time management techniques and strategies, you can reduce stress, improve your work-life balance, and enhance your mental health.

Quality and Innovation

Quality and Innovation are two concepts closely linked to improving processes, products, and services. They play a significant role in various fields, including business, technology, and healthcare, and can have a positive impact on mental health indirectly by creating a sense of accomplishment and job satisfaction.

Origins of Quality and Innovation:
1. **Quality:** The concept of quality has age-old origins, but it gained prominence during the Industrial Revolution when manufacturing standards and consistency became essential. In the mid-20th century, quality management approaches such as Total Quality Management (TQM) and Six Sigma were developed to ensure product and service excellence.
2. **Innovation:** Innovation has always been a driver of progress and development, from the invention of the wheel, to modern technological advancements. The term "innovation" gained significant attention in the business world during the late 20th century as companies recognized the need for continuous improvement and adaptation in a rapidly changing environment.

Here's a few examples:
1. **Quality:**
   - **Manufacturing:** In an automobile manufacturing plant, quality assurance measures ensure that each vehicle meets specific

standards and specifications, reducing defects and improving customer satisfaction.

- **Healthcare:** Medical devices, pharmaceuticals, and patient care services must meet rigorous quality standards to ensure patient safety and treatment effectiveness.
- **Software Development:** In software engineering, quality assurance involves rigorous testing and debugging to minimize errors and deliver a reliable product.

2. Innovation:

- **Technology:** Innovations like smartphones, artificial intelligence, and the internet have transformed our lives. The introduction of new features, functions, and products in the technology sector is driven by continuous innovation.
- **Healthcare:** Innovations in medical research and technology have led to breakthroughs in treatments, diagnostic tools, and healthcare management, improving patient outcomes and quality of life.
- **Business:** Innovative business models and marketing strategies have revolutionized the way companies operate and interact with customers.

How Quality and Innovation can improve your Mental Health:

1. **Sense of Accomplishment:** Working on projects that prioritize quality and innovation can provide a sense of accomplishment and pride in one's work, which is known to boost mental wellness.
2. **Job Satisfaction:** Quality and innovation contribute to job satisfaction. Employees who are part of a workplace that values these concepts are more likely to feel fulfilled in their roles, leading to reduced stress and increased mental health.
3. **Reduced Stress:** Ensuring quality in processes and products can reduce stress by preventing costly errors, rework, and customer complaints. Innovations can lead to more efficient and less stressful workflows.
4. **Adaptability:** Embracing innovation encourages adaptability and a growth mindset. People who are open to change and new ideas tend to have improved mental resilience and flexibility.

5. **Continuous Improvement:** Quality and innovation involve continuous learning and adaptation. Engaging in these processes can boost cognitive skills and mental agility.
6. **Positive Feedback Loop:** Quality and innovation often lead to positive feedback and recognition from peers and superiors, which can enhance self-esteem and mental wellness.
7. **Enhanced Creativity:** Innovation encourages creative thinking, and engaging in creative activities is known to reduce stress and improve mental health.

While quality and innovation directly impact various industries and processes, they can also have positive indirect effects on individuals' mental health by fostering a sense of achievement, job satisfaction, and adaptability in a dynamic and ever-evolving world.

So, what methods can you begin using to improve your quality and innovation within a working environment?

Here's some examples:
1. **Continuous Learning:**
   - Attend workshops, seminars, and online courses to acquire new skills and knowledge relevant to your field.
   - Stay up to date with industry trends, emerging technologies, and best practices.
2. **Networking:**
   - Engage with peers, mentors, and industry experts to exchange ideas and gain fresh perspectives.
   - Collaborate with colleagues on cross-functional projects to encourage innovative thinking.
3. **Feedback and Evaluation:**
   - Seek constructive feedback from supervisors and peers to identify areas for improvement.
   - Regularly assess your own work to spot opportunities for enhancing quality and innovation.
4. **Creative Problem-Solving:**
   - Encourage creative problem-solving by exploring various solutions to challenges.

- Use techniques like brainstorming, mind mapping, or the "Five Whys" method to delve deeper into issues.

5. **Quality Assurance:**
   - Develop or follow quality control processes to ensure that your work consistently meets high standards.
   - Implement key performance indicators (KPIs) and metrics to track quality and performance.

6. **Innovation Teams:**
   - Join or establish innovation teams or task forces within your organization to work on specific projects or initiatives.
   - Encourage a culture of innovation by proposing and supporting new ideas.

7. **Customer Feedback:**
   - Actively seek and consider customer feedback to identify areas for improvement.
   - Use customer input to drive product or service enhancements.

8. **Time Management:**
   - Efficiently manage your time to allocate more focused periods for innovative thinking and problem-solving.
   - Use time management techniques such as the Eisenhower Matrix to prioritize tasks.

9. **Experimentation:**
   - Be open to experimentation in your work. Try out new approaches, tools, or methodologies to find more effective solutions.
   - Keep records of your experiments and their outcomes.

10. **Mentorship:**
    - Seek mentorship from experienced colleagues or mentors who can guide you in quality improvement and innovative thinking.
    - Mentor others to share your knowledge and encourage a culture of learning and innovation.

11. **Innovation Tools and Techniques:**
    - Familiarize yourself with innovation frameworks like design thinking, Lean Startup, or Six Sigma.
    - Implement these methodologies in your projects to foster innovative problem-solving and quality enhancement.

12. Communication:
- Foster open and clear communication with team members and collaborators to share innovative ideas and best practices.
- Document your work and share it with others to promote knowledge sharing.

13. Cross-Functional Collaboration:
- Collaborate with colleagues from different departments and backgrounds to leverage diverse perspectives and foster innovation.
- Conduct interdepartmental workshops and brainstorming sessions.

14. Celebrate Success:
- Recognize and celebrate achievements, both big and small, to motivate yourself and your team.
- Share success stories and the lessons learned from innovative projects.

15. Personal Development Plan:
- Develop a personal development plan with specific goals related to quality and innovation.
- Regularly review and update your plan to stay on track and adapt to changing circumstances.

Improving quality and innovation in the workplace is an ongoing process that requires commitment, curiosity, and a willingness to embrace change. These examples can help you, and others around you, develop a mindset and approach that fosters continuous improvement and creativity.

Technological Integration:

Technological Integration refers to the incorporation and seamless use of various technologies and digital tools within a specific environment, such as a business, educational institution, or personal life. This integration aims to enhance efficiency, connectivity, and the ability to access and manipulate information, ultimately improving productivity and overall experiences. While the concept itself doesn't have a single point of origin, it gained prominence in the late 20th and early 21st centuries as technology became increasingly prevalent in everyday life. Here's some examples:

1. **Businesses:**
   - **Customer Relationship Management (CRM) Systems:** Businesses integrate CRM software to manage customer interactions, track sales leads, and improve customer service. This leads to better customer engagement, more effective marketing, and increased sales.
   - **Enterprise Resource Planning (ERP) Systems:** ERPs are integrated software solutions that help organizations manage various aspects of their operations, including finances, human resources, and supply chain. They optimize business processes, reduce manual work, and enhance data-driven decision-making.
2. **Education:**
   - **Learning Management Systems (LMS):** Educational institutions integrate LMS platforms to manage and deliver

course content, engage students, and track progress. This enhances learning experiences and provides valuable insights into student performance.

- **Digital Libraries:** Integrating digital libraries into the educational environment allows students to access a wide range of resources and information, promoting research and knowledge acquisition.

3. **Healthcare:**
- **Electronic Health Records (EHR):** Healthcare facilities integrate EHR systems to manage patient information and improve patient care through accurate and accessible medical records.
- **Telemedicine:** The integration of telemedicine platforms allows remote patient consultations, enhancing access to healthcare services, particularly in rural or underserved areas.

4. **Personal Life:**
- **Smart Home Systems:** Individuals integrate smart devices and systems in their homes, allowing them to control lighting, heating, and security remotely. This improves convenience and can contribute to peace of mind.
- **Health and Fitness Apps:** Many people integrate health and fitness apps and wearable devices to track their physical activity, nutrition, and health metrics, which can positively impact mental health through improved self-care.

How Technological Integration can improve your Mental Health:

1. **Convenience and Efficiency:** By automating repetitive tasks and streamlining processes, technological integration can reduce stress and save time, contributing to improved mental wellness.

2. **Access to Information:** Technology integration provides easy access to information and resources, which can empower individuals to make informed decisions and expand their knowledge.

3. **Enhanced Communication:** Integration tools like video conferencing and messaging apps foster better communication and social connections, especially important during times of remote work and social distancing.

4. **Telehealth Services:** The integration of telehealth platforms ensures individuals can access mental health services and support when needed, improving access and reducing barriers to care.
5. **Personalization:** Many integrated systems provide personalized experiences, tailoring content and services to individual preferences and needs, which can enhance satisfaction and reduce stress.
6. **Remote Work and Work-Life Balance:** For those who can work remotely, technological integration can enable more flexible work arrangements, improving work-life balance and reducing the stress associated with long commutes and rigid work schedules.
7. **Self-Management:** Health and wellness apps can help individuals track and manage their physical and mental health, promoting a sense of control and wellness.
8. **Connectedness:** Technology integration facilitates social connections, even at a distance, which is crucial for mental health, as social support and interactions contribute to wellness.

While technological integration can offer numerous benefits for mental health, it's essential to use technology mindfully and strike a balance to avoid potential negative effects, such as information overload and excessive screen time.

Work-Life Balance

Work-life balance is the equilibrium between the time and energy dedicated to one's professional life (work) and their personal life (family, hobbies, relaxation). It entails managing and prioritizing both aspects to ensure that neither excessively encroaches on the other. The concept originated as societal and workplace changes led to a growing awareness of the need to balance the demands of work and personal life.

Origins of Work-Life Balance:

The concept of work-life balance gained traction in the mid-20th century, primarily in response to significant societal changes and shifts in workplace culture. Historically, the boundary between work and personal life was less defined, and many people worked long hours with little time for leisure or family. The idea of work-life balance emerged as more women entered the workforce, and people sought to create a healthier separation between work and personal life. So, let's have a look at some strategies that you can employ to successfully achieve a healthy work-life balance.

1. **Flexible Work Hours:** Many companies now offer flexible work hours, allowing employees to adapt their schedules to better accommodate personal responsibilities. For instance, a parent may start, and finish work earlier to spend more time with their children.

2. **Remote Work:** The rise of remote work allows individuals to work from home or other locations, reducing commute times and enhancing work-life balance. This provides more opportunities for personal activities and family time.
3. **Paid Time Off:** Paid time off policies, such as vacation days and sick leave, support work-life balance by providing opportunities for rest, relaxation, and family activities.
4. **Technology for Remote Communication:** Communication tools like video conferencing and messaging apps enable work to continue while employees are away from the office, maintaining productivity without requiring a physical presence.
5. **Company Policies:** Many organizations now have policies that encourage work-life balance, such as no-work weekends, mental health days, or limits on overtime.

How a healthy Work-Life Balance can improve your Mental Health:
1. **Stress Reduction:** Balancing work and personal life can reduce chronic stress, which is a significant contributor to mental health issues like anxiety and depression.
2. **Increased Quality of Life:** More time spent on personal and leisure activities enhances overall wellness and life satisfaction.
3. **Better Physical Health:** Work-life balance allows individuals to prioritize self-care, including exercise, healthy eating, and adequate sleep, which are essential for mental and physical health.
4. **Stronger Relationships:** Time spent with family and friends' nurtures relationships, providing emotional support and reducing feelings of isolation or loneliness.
5. **Productivity and Creativity:** Balanced individuals tend to be more productive and creative at work, as they are refreshed and focused due to a well-balanced life.
6. **Improved Job Satisfaction:** When employees have a better work-life balance, they tend to be more satisfied in their jobs, which can reduce workplace stress and improve overall mental health.
7. **Personal Growth:** Balancing work and personal life enables personal growth, self-discovery, and the pursuit of interests and hobbies, all of which contribute to a sense of fulfilment.

8. **Resilience:** Maintaining a work-life balance can build resilience, making it easier to cope with challenges and adversity.
9. **Better Time Management:** Managing one's time between work and personal life promotes good time management skills, which can reduce stress and improve efficiency in both areas.

In conclusion, work-life balance is vital for maintaining and improving mental health. It helps reduce stress, fosters emotional wellness, strengthens relationships, and allows individuals to lead more satisfying and fulfilling lives by achieving a harmonious integration of work and personal life.

Personal Development

Personal development refers to the lifelong process of enhancing and nurturing one's skills, knowledge, character, and overall potential. It involves self-improvement in various aspects of life, including career, education, relationships, and personal wellness. Personal development is a deliberate and ongoing effort to grow, adapt, and evolve as an individual. While the concept has ancient philosophical and religious roots, the term "personal development" became more widespread in the 20th century as a response to societal and individual needs for self-improvement.

Origins of Personal Development:

The idea of personal development has been around for centuries, with roots in philosophy, psychology, and religious teachings. In ancient Greece, philosophers like *Socrates* emphasized self-examination and the pursuit of wisdom. The 19th and 20th centuries saw the emergence of self-help literature and movements, with authors like *Dale Carnegie* and *Napoleon Hill* promoting self-improvement. The term "personal development" became more commonly used in the late 20th century as a broader, holistic approach to self-improvement.

Here's some examples of how you can continue to develop yourself:
1. **Education and Skill Development:** Pursuing further education, acquiring new skills (e.g., learning a new language or mastering a musical instrument), and attending workshops or courses to enhance professional skills.

2. **Physical Health and Wellness:** Focusing on physical fitness, nutrition, and overall health, such as following a workout regimen, practicing yoga, or adopting a healthier diet.

3. **Emotional Intelligence:** Developing emotional intelligence by improving self-awareness, self-regulation, empathy, and interpersonal skills to build healthier relationships and manage emotions effectively.

4. **Career Advancement:** Advancing one's career through goal setting, networking, and improving job-related skills or seeking opportunities for professional growth.

5. **Personal Finance:** Managing personal finances, creating a budget, saving for the future, and investing to secure financial stability.

6. **Mental Health and Resilience:** Enhancing mental health through practices like mindfulness, meditation, cognitive-behavioural therapy, and other techniques that promote emotional wellness and resilience.

7. **Self-Reflection and Goal Setting:** Reflecting on personal values, setting goals, and creating a vision for the future to guide personal development efforts.

8. **Hobbies and Interests:** Exploring hobbies and interests, which can be intellectually stimulating and emotionally fulfilling, such as painting, reading, or gardening.

How Personal Development can improve your Mental Health:

1. **Increased Self-Esteem:** Achieving personal development goals can boost self-esteem and self-worth, leading to a more positive self-image and better mental health.

2. **Stress Reduction:** Techniques like mindfulness and emotional self-regulation, often included in personal development practices, can reduce stress and anxiety.

3. **Enhanced Coping Skills:** Personal development fosters resilience and equips individuals with better coping mechanisms to handle life's challenges and setbacks.

4. **Positive Mindset:** Engaging in personal development encourages a positive mindset, which can contribute to improved mental health and a more optimistic outlook on life.

5. **Goal Attainment:** Setting and achieving personal development goals fosters a sense of accomplishment, which can improve self-confidence and reduce feelings of inadequacy.
6. **Better Relationships:** Improving interpersonal skills and emotional intelligence can lead to healthier relationships, reducing conflict and improving overall mental wellness.
7. **Increased Fulfilment:** Pursuing personal interests and passions can bring joy and fulfilment, which is closely tied to mental health.
8. **Sense of Purpose:** Personal development can help individuals discover their purpose in life, providing motivation and a sense of direction that positively impacts mental health.

In summary, personal development is an ongoing journey of self-improvement that can significantly enhance mental health. By focusing on various aspects of personal growth and wellness, you can build resilience, self-esteem, and coping skills, leading to greater mental and emotional wellness.

Sustainability

Sustainability refers to the responsible and balanced use of resources and the long-term maintenance of ecological, economic, and social systems to meet current needs without compromising the ability of future generations to meet their needs. It involves considering the environmental impact of actions, the efficient use of resources, and the promotion of social equity and wellness. Sustainability has its roots in ecological science, ethical considerations, and social awareness.

Origins of Sustainability:

The concept of sustainability has deep historical and cultural roots, but it gained recognition in the 20th century as a result of growing concerns about environmental degradation, resource depletion, and social inequalities. It emerged from discussions on environmental ethics, ecological economics, and social justice. The term was popularized in 1987 with the publication of the '*Brundtland Report by the United Nations World Commission on Environment and Development*'.

Here's some examples of the different types of sustainability:

1. **Environmental Sustainability:** This involves practices that reduce harm to the environment and conserve natural resources. Examples include:

    - **Renewable Energy:** Using solar panels and wind turbines to generate clean energy.

- **Recycling and Waste Reduction:** Recycling materials and minimizing waste to reduce the environmental impact.

2. **Economic Sustainability:** Ensuring economic practices are viable in the long term without depleting resources or causing harm to communities. Examples include:
   - **Local Agriculture:** Supporting local agriculture to reduce the carbon footprint associated with food transportation.
   - **Ethical Investing:** Investing in companies with strong social and environmental practices.

3. **Social Sustainability:** Focusing on the wellness and equity of communities. Examples include:
   - **Affordable Housing:** Ensuring access to affordable and safe housing for all members of a community.
   - **Access to Healthcare:** Ensuring equitable access to healthcare services for all citizens.

4. **Personal Lifestyle:** Embracing sustainability in one's personal life by making environmentally conscious choices. Examples include:
   - **Reducing Carbon Footprint:** Using public transport, biking, or carpooling to reduce carbon emissions.
   - **Reducing Single-Use Plastics:** Minimizing the use of single-use plastics, such as plastic bags and bottles.

How being more sustainable can improve your Mental Health:

1. **Reduced Environmental Stress:** Sustainable practices that protect the environment can reduce the anxiety and stress associated with climate change and environmental degradation.

2. **Community Engagement:** Engaging in sustainability initiatives, such as local community gardens or conservation efforts, fosters a sense of belonging and community, contributing to improved mental wellness.

3. **Purpose and Meaning:** Embracing sustainability often provides individuals with a sense of purpose and meaning, which can enhance overall mental health and wellness.

4. **Resilience:** Sustainability practices, such as disaster preparedness and community support, can enhance resilience, reducing stress during times of crisis.

5. **Healthy Living:** Sustainable lifestyle choices, such as consuming locally sourced and organic foods, can improve physical health, which, in turn, contributes to better mental health.
6. **Connectedness:** Sustainability often involves connecting with nature, such as spending time outdoors and engaging in eco-friendly activities, which can reduce stress and improve mental health.
7. **Empowerment:** Participating in sustainability initiatives can empower individuals, giving them a sense of control over environmental and social issues, which can reduce feelings of helplessness.

Sustainability goes beyond environmental considerations; it encompasses social and economic aspects, making it a holistic approach to improving overall wellness. By promoting sustainable practices and behaviours, individuals and communities can contribute to a healthier and more balanced world, which can positively impact mental health.

Chapter 3

Time Management and Prioritization

Time is a limited resource, and how you use it has a direct impact on your productivity. We will explore effective time management techniques and how to prioritize tasks. I'll also provide tools and strategies for better managing your daily schedule.

The link between time management, prioritization, and mental health is well-established, and there is scientific evidence to support this connection.

Here's an exploration of this link and the science behind how managing time can reduce stress and anxiety:

1. **Cognitive Load and Stress Reduction:**
   - **Science:** When people have too many tasks and deadlines to manage simultaneously, their cognitive load increases. High cognitive load can lead to stress, anxiety, and reduced mental wellness. Research published in the '*Journal of Applied Psychology' (2007)* shows that task overload can negatively affect psychological wellness.
   - **Explanation:** Effective time management and prioritization help individuals avoid task overload. By allocating time and resources to tasks based on their importance and deadlines, people reduce cognitive load, which, in turn, lowers stress and anxiety levels.

2. **Sense of Control and Anxiety Reduction:**
   - **Science:** A study published in the *'National Institute of Health' (2018)* found that individuals with good time management skills reported lower anxiety levels. The study emphasized that perceived control over one's time and tasks significantly reduced anxiety.
   - **Explanation:** Time management provides individuals with a sense of control over their responsibilities. When they can plan, allocate time, and meet deadlines, it reduces the uncertainty and chaos often associated with unmanaged time, thereby reducing anxiety.

3. **Procrastination and Stress:**
   - **Science:** Procrastination, often linked to poor time management, has been found to increase stress. Research published in the *'National Library of Medicine' (2018)* indicates that procrastination can lead to chronic stress and poor psychological wellness.
   - **Explanation:** Effective time management and prioritization techniques can help individuals overcome procrastination by breaking tasks into manageable steps and allocating time to tackle them. This minimizes the stress that often results from procrastination.

4. **Work-Life Balance and Psychological Health:**
   - **Science:** Poor work-life balance, often a consequence of inadequate time management, has been linked to higher levels of stress, burnout, and mental health issues. Research in the *'Journal of Positive Psychology' (2015)* highlights the impact of work-life balance on psychological health.
   - **Explanation:** Effective time management allows individuals to allocate time to both work and personal life, reducing the stress associated with overworking and neglecting personal wellness.

5. **Achievement and Self-Esteem:**
   - **Science:** Accomplishing tasks and meeting deadlines, which are outcomes of effective time management, can boost self-esteem and overall wellness. Research published in the *'American*

Psychology Association' (2006) suggests that self-esteem is closely tied to achievement.

- **Explanation:** When individuals effectively manage their time and complete tasks, it leads to a sense of accomplishment. This, in turn, enhances self-esteem and reduces stress and anxiety related to feelings of inadequacy.

6. **Mindfulness and Time Management:**
   - **Science:** Mindfulness practices, which are often incorporated into time management techniques, have been shown to reduce stress and anxiety. Research in the *'Journal of Anxiety, Stress & Coping' (2016)* demonstrates that mindfulness practices can reduce stress.
   - **Explanation:** Time management techniques like time blocking and prioritization require focused attention and presence in the moment. This aligns with the principles of mindfulness, promoting reduced stress and enhanced wellness.

Scientific studies and research findings consistently demonstrate the positive impact of effective time management and prioritization on reducing stress and anxiety. By managing time wisely, individuals gain a sense of control, reduce cognitive load, overcome procrastination, and improve their work-life balance, leading to enhanced mental health and overall wellness.

Certainly, there are various tools and strategies available to help individuals better manage their daily schedules and improve their time management.

Here are some examples. Some of the tools that we will be delving deeper in to are:

1. **Calendar Apps:** Calendar apps like Google Calendar, Apple Calendar, or Microsoft Outlook allow you to schedule and organize your daily activities. They can send reminders and notifications to keep you on track.
2. **Task Management Apps:** Apps like Todoist, Trello, or Asana enable you to create task lists, set priorities, and track progress on various projects and responsibilities.
3. **Time Tracking Software:** Tools like Toggl or RescueTime help

you monitor how you spend your time, allowing you to identify productivity patterns and areas for improvement.

4. **Time Blocking:** Use a planner or calendar to allocate specific blocks of time for different tasks. This technique helps you stay focused and organized.

5. **Note-Taking Apps:** Apps like Evernote or Microsoft OneNote can help you jot down ideas, tasks, and notes on the go, ensuring you don't forget important details.

6. **To-Do Lists:** Traditional to-do lists, whether written on paper or in digital format, are simple yet effective tools for tracking and prioritizing daily tasks.

7. **Productivity Apps:** Apps like **ProductivityGo** offer courses which enable you to unlock your productivity potential.

Strategies that are worth learning and employing into your daily habits include:

1. **Prioritization:** Use techniques like the Eisenhower Matrix (quadrant method) to categorize tasks into urgent and important, allowing you to focus on the most critical ones first.

2. **Time Management Techniques:** Explore methods like the Pomodoro Technique (working in focused intervals) or the 2-Minute Rule (tackle tasks that take less than 2 minutes immediately) to improve efficiency.

3. **Batching Tasks:** Group similar tasks together and tackle them in a single time block. For example, set aside a block for answering emails or making phone calls.

4. **Set Clear Goals:** Define clear, achievable goals for the day. Knowing what you want to accomplish makes it easier to structure your schedule.

5. **Plan the Night Before:** Spend a few minutes at the end of each day planning the next. This allows you to start your day with a clear direction.

6. **Limit Distractions:** Identify common distractions and create strategies to minimize them, such as turning off notifications during focused work.

7. **Regular Breaks:** Schedule short breaks between tasks to recharge

your energy and maintain focus throughout the day.

8. **Delegate and Outsource:** If possible, delegate tasks to others or outsource non-essential activities to free up your time for higher-priority work.

9. **Flexibility:** Be open to adjustments in your schedule. Unexpected events can occur, so the ability to adapt is crucial.

10. **Time Audit:** Periodically review how you spend your time to identify inefficiencies and areas where you can make improvements.

11. **Goal Setting:** Define long-term and short-term goals for your personal and professional life. Your daily schedule should align with these goals.

12. **No Multitasking:** Focus on one task at a time. Multitasking can decrease productivity and increase stress.

13. **Self-Care Time:** Allocate time for self-care activities, whether it's exercise, meditation, or pursuing hobbies. Maintaining a work-life balance is vital for overall wellness.

Remember that the effectiveness of these tools and strategies can vary depending on individual preferences and needs. Experiment with different approaches to find the combination that works best for you in managing your daily schedule.

Calendar Apps

A calendar app, short for calendar application, is a software tool or mobile application that allows users to create, manage, and track events, appointments, and tasks on a digital calendar. It serves as a digital representation of a traditional paper calendar, but with added functionality and features to help users stay organized. Calendar apps have become integral to managing personal and professional schedules, improving productivity, and reducing stress and mental clutter.

Origins of Calendar Apps:

The concept of electronic calendars can be traced back to the early days of personal computers, where rudimentary calendar functions were built into operating systems or offered as standalone software. However, it was the advent of smartphones and the development of app ecosystems that popularized and refined calendar apps. Apple's introduction of the iPhone in 2007 and Google's development of Google Calendar were instrumental in bringing digital calendars to a broader audience.

Examples of Calendar Apps:

1. **Google Calendar:** One of the most widely used calendar apps, Google Calendar offers features like event creation, reminders, and integration with other Google services. It's accessible on various platforms and devices.

2. **Apple Calendar (formerly iCal):** Built into Apple's macOS and iOS ecosystems, Apple Calendar provides a user-friendly interface and seamless integration with other Apple services like iCloud.

3. **Microsoft Outlook:** Part of the Microsoft Office suite, Outlook's calendar app is favoured for its robust scheduling and email integration features, making it popular in professional settings.

4. **Calendly:** A specialized calendar app for scheduling appointments and meetings. It simplifies the process of setting up meetings, interviews, or consultations by allowing others to book time slots in your calendar.

How Calendar Apps can improve Mental Health and Productivity:

1. **Reduced Cognitive Load:** Calendar apps help individuals offload the mental burden of remembering important dates, deadlines, and appointments. This reduces cognitive load and mental clutter, leading to less stress and anxiety.

2. **Time Management:** Calendar apps enable effective time management by allowing users to allocate time for tasks and appointments. This structured approach reduces the stress associated with missed deadlines or overcommitting.

3. **Organization and Prioritization:** Users can categorize events, tasks, and appointments, helping them prioritize and organize their schedules. This promotes better decision-making and reduces the mental strain of figuring out what to do next.

4. **Set Reminders:** Calendar apps send notifications and reminders for upcoming events, reducing the stress of forgetting critical tasks or appointments.

5. **Increased Productivity:** By streamlining daily schedules, calendar apps help individuals allocate time to important tasks, ensuring they stay on track and make the most of their time.

6. **Improved Work-Life Balance:** Calendar apps can help individuals allocate time for personal activities and self-care. This supports a healthier work-life balance, which is crucial for overall mental wellness.

7. **Collaboration and Communication:** Many calendar apps allow for sharing and collaborative scheduling, reducing misunderstandings and conflicts related to appointments or meetings. This leads to smoother interactions and lower stress levels.
8. **Data Insights:** Calendar apps often provide insights into how time is spent, helping individuals identify areas where they can improve efficiency and reduce stress-inducing bottlenecks.

In conclusion, calendar apps have become indispensable tools for managing daily schedules and improving mental health and productivity. They offer a structured approach to time management, reducing stress by helping users stay organized, prioritize tasks, and stay on top of their commitments.

Task Management Apps

A task management app is a software tool or mobile application designed to help individuals or teams organize, track, and prioritize tasks and activities. These apps are used to create to-do lists, set deadlines, and manage the completion of tasks efficiently. Task management apps provide a structured way to stay on top of work and personal responsibilities, improving productivity and reducing stress associated with disorganization.

Origins of Task Management Apps:

The concept of task management and to-do lists has a long history, dating back to handwritten lists and rudimentary task management tools. The digital task management app, as we know it today, emerged with the growth of personal computing and mobile technology. It was further popularized by the need for digital organization in both professional and personal contexts.

Examples of Task Management Apps:

1. **Todoist:** A popular and user-friendly task management app that allows users to create, prioritize, and organize tasks. It offers features like due dates, recurring tasks, and project organization.

2. **Wunderlist (now Microsoft To Do):** Known for its simplicity and collaborative features, Wunderlist allowed users to create and share lists, set due dates, and attach files. It was later integrated into Microsoft's task management ecosystem.

3. **Trello:** A visual project management tool that uses boards, lists, and cards to help users organize tasks and projects. Trello is especially useful for teams working collaboratively.
4. **Microsoft To Do:** Microsoft's task management app that integrates with other Microsoft products, such as Outlook and Microsoft Office. It offers features like task lists, due dates, and integration with your calendar.
5. **Asana:** A task and project management app favoured by teams and professionals. Asana allows for task assignment, project tracking, and collaboration with team members.

How Task Management Apps can improve Mental Health and Productivity:
1. **Reduced Mental Clutter:** Task management apps help individuals offload mental clutter by providing a place to record and organize tasks. This reduces the mental stress associated with trying to remember everything.
2. **Organization and Prioritization:** Task management apps enable users to categorize, prioritize, and structure their tasks. This promotes effective decision-making and helps reduce stress associated with feeling overwhelmed.
3. **Time Management:** These apps often include due dates and reminders, helping users allocate time for tasks and deadlines. Effective time management reduces stress related to last-minute rushes.
4. **Collaboration and Communication:** Many task management apps support team collaboration. Clear task assignment and communication features reduce misunderstandings and conflicts, contributing to reduced stress and enhanced productivity.
5. **Progress Tracking:** Users can track the completion of tasks, providing a sense of accomplishment and reducing stress associated with feeling unproductive.
6. **Accountability:** Task management apps can create a sense of accountability. Knowing that tasks are tracked and visible to others can motivate individuals to stay productive, reducing procrastination and associated stress.

7. **Goal Achievement:** Task management apps help users set and achieve goals, whether they are work-related or personal. This sense of accomplishment enhances self-esteem and reduces stress.

8. **Focus on Important Tasks:** By helping individuals identify and prioritize important tasks, these apps reduce the stress of juggling multiple responsibilities and ensure that critical tasks receive attention.

Task management apps offer a structured and effective way to stay organized and reduce the mental clutter associated with disorganization. They provide tools for managing tasks, setting priorities, and tracking progress, ultimately improving productivity and mental wellness.

Time Tracking Software

Time tracking software is a computer-based tool or application that allows individuals or organizations to monitor and record the time spent on tasks, projects, or activities. These tools help users gain insights into how they allocate their time, track productivity, and identify areas for improvement. Time tracking software is used across various industries to enhance productivity and reduce stress by providing a structured way to manage time.

Origins of Time Tracking Software:

The concept of time tracking can be traced back to the early days of project management and workforce management, where primitive methods like paper timesheets and punch cards were used to record working hours. With the advent of digital technology, time tracking software emerged as a more efficient and accurate way to monitor time usage. Early software solutions were introduced in the 1990s, and the field has continued to evolve with the development of more advanced tools.

Examples of Time Tracking Software:

1. **Toggl:** Toggl is a popular time tracking tool that offers a simple and user-friendly interface. Users can track time for various tasks and projects, generate reports, and analyse time data.
2. **Harvest:** Harvest is a time tracking and invoicing tool that allows users to monitor time spent on projects and create invoices based on the tracked hours.

3. **RescueTime:** RescueTime runs in the background and tracks time spent on various applications and websites. It provides insights into how users allocate their digital time.
4. **Clockify:** Clockify is a versatile time tracking tool that offers features like timesheets, project tracking, and reporting. It can be used for personal time tracking and team collaboration.
5. **Hubstaff:** Hubstaff is a time tracking and employee monitoring tool designed for businesses. It tracks time, monitors productivity, and helps manage remote teams.

How Time Tracking Software can improve Mental Health and Productivity:
1. **Awareness of Time Usage:** Time tracking software helps users become aware of how they spend their time. This awareness can lead to better time management and reduced stress.
2. **Productivity Insights:** By monitoring time spent on tasks and projects, users can identify inefficiencies, distractions, and time-wasting activities. This insight can lead to more productive work habits.
3. **Goal Setting and Achievement:** Time tracking software enables users to set time-based goals and track their progress. Achieving these goals can boost self-esteem and reduce stress.
4. **Prioritization:** Users can allocate time to essential tasks and prioritize work based on tracked data. This reduces the stress associated with juggling numerous responsibilities.
5. **Time Management:** Time tracking software can encourage better time management by prompting users to allocate time for tasks and adhere to schedules.
6. **Elimination of Unnecessary Tasks:** By identifying tasks that consume excessive time with little value, users can eliminate or delegate them, reducing the stress of unproductive work.
7. **Work-Life Balance:** Time tracking can help individuals allocate time for personal activities, hobbies, and self-care, promoting a healthier work-life balance.

8. **Accountability:** For teams, time tracking can create a sense of accountability and transparency, leading to improved collaboration and reduced stress associated with miscommunications.

In summary, time tracking software offers a structured and data-driven approach to managing time, which can significantly improve mental health and productivity. By providing insights into time usage and promoting efficient work habits, it helps users reduce stress and achieve a better work-life balance.

Time Blocking

Time blocking is a time management technique that involves scheduling specific blocks of time for focused work on particular tasks, projects, or activities. It is a proactive approach to managing one's schedule by allocating time in advance for essential or priority work. Time blocking helps individuals stay organized, manage their tasks efficiently, and improve productivity.

Origins of Time Blocking:

Time blocking has its roots in various time management and productivity philosophies, with influences from methods like the Pomodoro Technique and personal productivity systems like Getting Things Done (GTD) by *David Allen*. The concept of setting aside dedicated time for tasks and avoiding interruptions is central to time blocking.

Examples of Time Blocking:
1. **Work Tasks:** A professional might use time blocking to allocate a specific block of time in the morning for focused work on a critical project, minimizing distractions during that time.
2. **Study Sessions:** Students can use time blocking to set aside chunks of time for studying, research, or completing assignments. For example, designating two hours in the evening for focused study.
3. **Meetings and Appointments:** Time blocking is useful for scheduling meetings, appointments, or consultations. This ensures that you have dedicated time for these activities without overlapping with other tasks.

4. **Personal Goals:** Time blocking can be applied to personal goals. For instance, allocating time each morning for exercise or meditation to prioritize physical and mental wellness.

5. **Household Chores:** Time blocking can help individuals manage household tasks efficiently. Setting aside time for cleaning, cooking, or home maintenance reduces stress associated with a disorganized home.

How Time Blocking can improve Productivity:
1. **Focused Work:** By dedicating uninterrupted time to specific tasks, time blocking encourages deep work and concentration. This results in more productive and efficient work.
2. **Prioritization:** Time blocking forces individuals to prioritize tasks and allocate time to what matters most. This prevents them from getting sidetracked by less important activities.
3. **Reduced Multitasking:** Multitasking can decrease productivity and increase stress. Time blocking promotes single-tasking, which is more effective and less stressful.
4. **Proactive Planning:** Time blocking involves planning your day or week in advance, allowing you to be more proactive and less reactive to disruptions.
5. **Effective Use of Time:** Time blocking ensures that each block of time has a clear purpose, reducing the stress of uncertainty about what to do next.
6. **Time Management:** This technique helps individuals manage their time effectively, ensuring that they make the most of their work hours and have time left for personal activities.

Time blocking is a powerful time management technique that can significantly improve productivity. It encourages focused, organized work, reduces stress by creating a structured schedule, and helps individuals manage their time effectively by prioritizing tasks and avoiding the pitfalls of multitasking.

Note-Taking Apps

Note-taking apps are software tools or applications designed for capturing and organizing notes, ideas, information, and data in digital format. These apps provide a convenient and efficient way to create, store, search, and manage notes, making it easier to access and reference information. Note-taking apps have become an integral part of personal and professional productivity, helping users stay organized and save time.

Origins of Note-Taking Apps:

The concept of note-taking predates digital technology and has been practiced for centuries. People traditionally took notes on paper, in journals, or on sticky notes. With the advent of computers and smartphones, the concept evolved into digital note-taking apps. Early examples included simple text editors and word processors. However, dedicated note-taking apps gained prominence in the mid-2000s with the emergence of mobile devices and app ecosystems.

Examples of Note-Taking Apps:
1. **Evernote:** Evernote is a versatile note-taking app that allows users to create, organize, and search for notes. It supports various media types, such as text, images, audio, and web clippings.
2. **OneNote:** Developed by Microsoft, OneNote is a digital notebook that integrates with the Microsoft Office suite. Users can create and organize notes in a notebook-style format.

3. **Google Keep:** Google Keep is a simple and user-friendly note-taking app that syncs with Google Drive. It offers features for creating notes, checklists, and voice recordings.
4. **Notion:** Notion is a comprehensive workspace tool that combines note-taking, project management, and databases. Users can create pages, databases, and templates to organize information.
5. **Simplenote:** As the name suggests, Simplenote is a straightforward note-taking app for text-based notes. It focuses on simplicity and fast synchronization.

How Note-Taking Apps can improve Time Management:
1. **Quick Capture:** Note-taking apps allow users to quickly jot down ideas, tasks, or information as they arise. This prevents important details from being forgotten and saves time that would otherwise be spent trying to recall them.
2. **Organized Information:** Note-taking apps provide a structured way to organize and categorize notes. This makes it easier to find and reference information, reducing the time spent searching for notes or documents.
3. **Task Lists:** Users can create to-do lists and task lists within note-taking apps. This helps with time management by keeping track of tasks, deadlines, and priorities.
4. **Centralized Storage:** Instead of scattering notes across various notebooks or devices, note-taking apps offer centralized storage. This ensures that all important information is accessible in one place, saving time otherwise wasted on searching.
5. **Synchronization:** Many note-taking apps offer synchronization across multiple devices, ensuring that notes are always up to date and accessible. This eliminates the need to manually transfer or email notes between devices.
6. **Reminders:** Some note-taking apps include reminder features, helping users manage their time effectively by setting deadlines or alarms for specific notes or tasks.
7. **Accessibility:** Digital notes can be accessed from anywhere with an internet connection. This flexibility enables users to manage their time efficiently while on the go.

8. **Collaboration:** Note-taking apps with collaboration features facilitate efficient sharing and teamwork, reducing the time needed for communication and document exchange.

Note-taking apps are valuable tools for improving time management. They streamline the process of capturing and organizing information, ensuring that users can quickly access notes, tasks, and ideas when needed. This organization reduces the time spent searching for information and supports effective time management by centralizing important details in one accessible location.

Productivity Apps

Productivity apps are software tools or applications designed to enhance an individual's or team's efficiency, time management, and output in various aspects of work and life. These apps provide features and functionalities that assist in organizing tasks, projects, schedules, and communication. Productivity apps have gained popularity with the growth of digital technology and have become essential tools for both personal and professional use. In late 2023, I created an app which teaches users to become more productive in their workplace, ultimately reducing the time spent working, and increasing time spent focusing on their mental wellness, fitness, family, and hobbies. The app is called 'ProductivityGo' and you should definitely head to the app stores and download it! The content included (for free) will change your life.

Origins of Productivity Apps:

The concept of productivity apps evolved with the rise of personal computing and the integration of digital technology into daily tasks. Early examples included rudimentary personal information managers (PIMs) that provided calendar and task management. Over time, these apps became more sophisticated, with mobile devices playing a significant role in making productivity apps accessible to a broader audience. The idea of having tools to streamline work and time management is rooted in long-standing productivity methodologies and philosophies, such as time management, GTD (Getting Things Done), and lean productivity principles.

Examples of Productivity Apps:
1. **ProductivityGo:** An app which delivers (in-app) courses, online events, as well as an online social experience and support with others who are working to unlock their full potential.
2. **Microsoft Office Suite:** Including apps like Microsoft Word, Excel, and PowerPoint, this suite is widely used for word processing, spreadsheet management, and presentation creation.
3. **Slack:** A team collaboration and communication app that offers channels, direct messaging, file sharing, and integrations with other productivity tools.
4. **Trello:** A visual project management tool that helps teams organize tasks and projects using boards, lists, and cards.
5. **Zoom:** A video conferencing and communication app that has gained popularity for remote work and online meetings.
6. **Todoist:** A task management app that allows users to create to-do lists, set deadlines, and prioritize tasks.
7. **Asana:** A project management and team collaboration tool designed to manage tasks, projects, and teams.
8. **Google Workspace (formerly G Suite):** A suite of productivity apps including Gmail, Google Docs, Google Sheets, and Google Calendar, among others, that supports collaboration and productivity in the cloud.

How Productivity Apps can improve Time Management:
1. **Task Management:** Productivity apps often include task and to-do list management features, helping users organize their work and allocate time to specific tasks.
2. **Scheduling:** Calendar and scheduling features in productivity apps enable users to allocate time for appointments, meetings, and tasks, promoting efficient time management.
3. **Automation:** Some productivity apps offer automation features that can save time by streamlining repetitive tasks and workflows.
4. **Communication:** Communication tools within productivity apps reduce the time needed for back-and-forth email communication or physical meetings.

5. **Collaboration:** Collaboration features in productivity apps allow teams to work together efficiently, reducing the time spent on coordinating and sharing information.
6. **File Management:** File sharing and storage capabilities in many productivity apps simplify document management and reduce time spent searching for files.
7. **Integration:** Productivity apps often integrate with other apps and services, providing a central hub for managing different tasks and reducing the time needed to switch between tools.
8. **Progress Tracking:** Many productivity apps offer tracking and reporting features, allowing users to monitor progress and make informed decisions about time allocation.

Productivity apps are designed to improve time management by offering a range of features and tools that streamline work processes, facilitate task management, enhance communication, and support collaboration. These apps can save time and enhance efficiency, making them essential for individuals and teams looking to optimize their productivity and time management.

Chapter 4

Goal Setting and Planning

The link between goal setting, planning, and mental health is a well-established and scientifically supported concept. Effective goal setting and planning can positively impact mental health by reducing stress and anxiety through several mechanisms:

1. **Clarity and Purpose:** Setting clear and achievable goals provides individuals with a sense of purpose and direction. This clarity reduces feelings of aimlessness and uncertainty, which can lead to anxiety and stress. Knowing what you want to achieve and having a plan to get there can create a sense of fulfilment and motivation.

2. **Stress Reduction:** When goals are well-defined and broken down into manageable steps, individuals can approach tasks in an organized and systematic way. This reduces the stress associated with feeling overwhelmed by a complex or ambiguous task.

3. **Empowerment:** Goal setting and planning empower individuals to take control of their lives and circumstances. This sense of control can be a significant buffer against stress and anxiety, as it fosters self-efficacy and resilience.

4. **Time Management:** Effective planning involves allocating time for tasks and setting priorities. This enhances time management skills and reduces the stress of missed deadlines and time-related pressure.

5. **Accomplishment and Self-Esteem:** Achieving set goals boosts self-esteem and self-worth. This sense of accomplishment has a direct impact on mental health by reducing self-doubt and anxiety.

6. **Adaptability:** Effective planning includes contingency planning and flexibility. Being prepared for potential setbacks or unexpected changes reduces the stress associated with unpredictability.

Scientific studies and research support the link between goal setting, planning, and improved mental health. For example:

- A study published in the '*American Journal of Lifestyle Medicine*' *(2017)* found that individuals who set clear, realistic goals for exercise and diet reported reduced stress and improved mental wellness.

- Research conducted by the '*Dominican University of California*' *(2023)* demonstrated that individuals who wrote down their goals and created specific action plans were more likely to achieve their goals and experience reduced stress compared to those who didn't engage in these practices.

Examples of Goal Setting and Planning Exercises:

1. **SMART Goals:** Use the SMART (Specific, Measurable, Achievable, Relevant, Time-bound) criteria to set clear and well-defined goals. For instance, if you want to reduce stress through exercise, your SMART goal might be, "I will walk for 30 minutes, five days a week, for the next three months."

2. **Prioritization:** Create a to-do list for the day or week and prioritize tasks based on importance and deadlines. Use a technique like the Eisenhower Matrix to categorize tasks as urgent, important, or neither.

3. **Mindfulness Planning:** Plan moments of mindfulness or meditation in your day to reduce stress. For example, set aside 10 minutes in the morning and evening for mindfulness exercises.

4. **Progress Tracking:** Create a visual representation of your goals and progress, such as a vision board or a goal journal. Document your achievements and setbacks to maintain motivation and adapt your plans as needed.

5. **Contingency Planning:** In your goal-setting and planning, consider potential obstacles and have a plan for dealing with them. For example, if your goal is to reduce clutter, plan for decluttering one room at a time and anticipate potential time constraints or emotional challenges.

6. **Self-Care Planning:** Make self-care a priority by scheduling time for activities that promote relaxation and wellness, such as taking a warm bath, reading, or spending quality time with loved ones.

The link between goal setting, planning, and mental health is grounded in scientific research. By setting clear and achievable goals, planning for their attainment, and effectively managing time, you can reduce stress and anxiety, enhance self-esteem, and improve your overall mental wellness. Goal setting and planning exercises provide practical strategies for applying these principles in daily life.

SMART Goals

A SMART goal is a specific, well-defined, and structured goal-setting framework that helps individuals and organizations set clear objectives. SMART is an acronym that stands for Specific, Measurable, Achievable, Relevant, and Time-bound. This framework provides a systematic approach to goal setting, making it easier to understand, track progress, and achieve success. SMART goals are widely used in various fields, from personal development to project management.

Origins of SMART Goals:

The SMART goal-setting concept has a history that can be traced back to the works of *George T. Doran*, who first introduced the acronym in a paper titled *"There's a S.M.A.R.T. Way to Write Management's Goals and Objectives"* published in the November 1981 issue of Management Review. The SMART acronym was created to help organizations and individuals create more effective goals.

SMART Goal Components:

1. **Specific:** A specific goal is clear, well-defined, and unambiguous. It answers the questions of who, what, where, when, and why. Specific goals focus on the most important aspects of the goal, avoiding vague or overly general language.
   - Example: "I will lose 10 pounds by jogging for 30 minutes every morning before work."

2. **Measurable:** A measurable goal includes criteria for tracking progress and determining when the goal is achieved. It allows you to quantify or measure your progress.
   - Example: "I will track my daily calorie intake and aim to consume no more than 1,800 calories per day."
3. **Achievable:** An achievable goal is realistic and attainable. It considers your resources, constraints, and capabilities. It should stretch your abilities but remain within the realm of possibility.
   - Example: "I will reduce my screen time to two hours per day, which is realistic given my work schedule and responsibilities."
4. **Relevant:** A relevant goal is aligned with your values, long-term objectives, and the context of your life. It ensures that the goal is worth pursuing and meaningful to you.
   - Example: "I will take an online course in project management, which is relevant to my career goals and professional development."
5. **Time-bound:** A time-bound goal has a defined time frame or deadline. It helps create a sense of urgency and sets a clear timeline for achieving the goal.
   - Example: "I will complete the first draft of my novel within six months."

How SMART Goals Improve Time Management:

1. **Clarity:** The specificity of SMART goals ensures that you clearly understand what needs to be done and when it needs to be completed. This clarity helps you manage your time effectively by focusing on the most important tasks.
2. **Prioritization:** SMART goals require you to determine the importance and relevance of your objectives, helping you prioritize tasks. This prevents time wasted on less crucial activities.
3. **Progress Tracking:** Measurable and time-bound elements enable you to track your progress. Regularly assessing your advancement helps you adjust your time management strategies and stay on track.
4. **Motivation:** Achievable and relevant components of SMART goals ensure that your objectives are realistic and personally meaningful.

This motivation can boost your time management efforts by keeping you committed to your goals.

5. **Deadline Focus:** Time-bound goals emphasize the importance of deadlines. This focus on timelines can enhance your time management skills by instilling a sense of urgency.

SMART goals are a practical and widely used framework for goal setting that promotes effective time management. By setting clear, specific, and achievable objectives with measurable and time-bound components, individuals can streamline their time management efforts, prioritize tasks, track progress, and maintain motivation toward their goals.

SMART Goal: Practice

S

1. Specific: A specific goal is clear, well-defined, and unambiguous. It answers the questions of who, what, where, when, and why.

M

2. Measurable: A measurable goal includes criteria for tracking progress and determining when the goal is achieved.

A

3. Achievable: An achievable goal is realistic and attainable. It considers your resources, constraints, and capabilities.

R

4. Relevant: A relevant goal is aligned with your values, long-term objectives, and the context of your life. It ensures that the goal is worth pursuing and meaningful to you.

T

5. Time-bound: A time-bound goal has a defined time frame or deadline. It helps create a sense of urgency and sets a clear timeline for achieving the goal.

Prioritization using the Eisenhower Matrix

The Eisenhower Matrix, also known as the Urgent-Important Matrix, is a time management and prioritization tool that helps individuals categorize tasks based on their urgency and importance. Here's a breakdown of the four quadrants and how to prioritize work using the Eisenhower Matrix:

Quadrant 1: Urgent and Important (Do First)

Tasks in this quadrant are both urgent and important, requiring immediate attention. They are critical to your success or the success of your project.

Examples:

- Meeting a tight deadline for a project.
- Resolving a critical issue that has arisen unexpectedly.
- Handling an urgent client request.

Quadrant 2: Not Urgent but Important (Schedule)

Tasks in this quadrant are important for your long-term goals and success but are not necessarily time-sensitive. Planning and scheduling these tasks is crucial for proactive and strategic work.

Examples:

- Long-term project planning.
- Skill development and training.
- Relationship building and networking.
- Strategic planning and goal setting.

Quadrant 3: Urgent but Not Important (Delegate)

Tasks in this quadrant are urgent but may not contribute significantly to your long-term goals. Delegating these tasks whenever possible is key to freeing up your time for more critical responsibilities.

Examples:

- Responding to non-critical emails or calls.
- Attending meetings that are not directly relevant to your core responsibilities.
- Handling routine administrative tasks.

Quadrant 4: Not Urgent and Not Important (Eliminate or Minimize)

Tasks in this quadrant are neither urgent nor important, and they can be a distraction from more critical activities. Consider eliminating or minimizing these tasks to focus on more valuable activities.

Examples:

- Excessive time spent on social media.
- Engaging in activities that don't contribute to personal or professional growth.
- Procrastinating or engaging in time-wasting activities.

Steps to Prioritize Using the Eisenhower Matrix:

1. **List Your Tasks:** Write down all the tasks you need to accomplish.
2. **Categorize Tasks:** Place each task in the appropriate quadrant based on its urgency and importance.
3. **Prioritize:** Start with tasks in Quadrant 1, as they require immediate attention. Move to Quadrant 2 for long-term planning and strategic activities. Delegate tasks in Quadrant 3 and consider eliminating or minimizing tasks in Quadrant 4.
4. **Create an Action Plan:** Develop a plan for addressing tasks in each quadrant. Schedule time for Quadrant 2 tasks, delegate tasks appropriately, and eliminate or minimize activities in Quadrant 4.
5. **Regularly Review and Adjust:** Periodically review and adjust your tasks as priorities may change. This ensures that you stay focused on what truly matters.

By consistently using the Eisenhower Matrix, you can become more strategic in your decision-making, focus on high-priority tasks, and achieve a better balance between urgency and importance in your work.

Progress Tracking

Tracking progress is crucial for personal and professional development. It helps individuals stay focused, motivated, and accountable for their goals. Here are several ways you can track your progress, along with examples:

1. Set Clear Goals:
- Example: Instead of a vague goal like "lose weight," set a specific goal like "lose 10 pounds in the next three months."

2. Break Down Goals into Milestones:
- Example: If the goal is to read 20 books in a year, break it down into monthly targets, aiming for about 2 books per month.

3. Use a Journal or Planner:
- Example: Keep a daily journal where you record tasks completed, challenges faced, and insights gained. Use a planner to schedule activities and track achievements.

4. Create a Task List:
- Example: Make a to-do list for the day or week, including both short-term and long-term tasks. Check off items as they are completed.

5. Utilize Project Management Tools:
- Example: Use tools like Trello, Asana, or Jira to organize tasks, set deadlines, and track progress on larger projects. These tools often provide visual representations of progress.

6. Visualize Progress with Charts:

- Example: Create a visual chart or graph to represent your progress. For instance, a bar chart showing the number of books read each month or a line graph tracking weight loss over time.

7. Keep a Habit Tracker:

- Example: Use a habit-tracking app or a simple chart to monitor daily habits. For instance, if the goal is to exercise regularly, mark each day on the tracker when the workout is completed.

8. Measure Key Performance Indicators (KPIs):

- Example: If the goal is to increase website traffic, regularly monitor KPIs such as page views, unique visitors, and bounce rates.

9. Reflect and Evaluate Regularly:

- Example: Schedule regular checkpoints to reflect on your progress. Ask questions like "What worked well?" and "What could be improved?" Adjust your approach accordingly.

10. Celebrate Achievements:

- Example: Acknowledge and celebrate milestones and achievements along the way. This could be a small reward for completing a challenging task or reaching a specific target.

11. Seek Feedback:

- Example: Request feedback from mentors, colleagues, or friends. Their insights can provide valuable perspectives on your progress and areas for improvement.

12. Use Personal Development Apps:

- Example: Explore apps designed for personal development and goal tracking, such as HabitBull, Strides, or MyFitnessPal, depending on the specific area of focus.

13. Track Financial Progress:

- Example: Keep a budget and track expenses to monitor financial goals. Use tools like Mint or YNAB to visualize spending habits and savings progress.

14. Maintain a Portfolio:

- Example: Create a portfolio to showcase your work and achievements, whether in the form of a physical portfolio, a personal website, or a LinkedIn profile.

15. Regularly Update Your Resume or CV:
- Example: Update your resume or CV periodically to reflect new skills acquired, projects completed, and achievements attained.

Remember that the key is to find methods that align with your preferences and the nature of your goals. Consistent tracking and evaluation will help you stay on course and make informed decisions to improve your performance over time.

Contingency Planning

Contingency planning is the process of developing strategies and actions to address potential events or situations that may disrupt normal operations or cause unforeseen challenges. The goal is to prepare for the unexpected, mitigate risks, and ensure that an organization, or individual, can respond effectively to various scenarios. Successful contingency planning involves identifying potential risks, developing response plans, and regularly reviewing and updating these plans. Here's a guide on how to achieve effective contingency planning, along with examples:

Steps to Achieve Contingency Planning:
  1. Risk Identification:
  - Identify potential risks that could impact your organization. These can include natural disasters, technological failures, supply chain disruptions, economic downturns, or other unexpected events.
  - Example: A retail business might identify supply chain interruptions due to a global pandemic or severe weather affecting product shipments.

  2. Impact Assessment:
  - Assess the potential impact of each identified risk on your organization. Consider the consequences in terms of operations, finances, reputation, and other critical areas.
  - Example: An online service provider may assess the impact of a cyberattack on customer data, potential downtime, and damage to the company's reputation.

3. Prioritization of Risks:
- Prioritize the identified risks based on their likelihood and potential impact. Focus on those with the highest severity and develop contingency plans accordingly.
- Example: A manufacturing company may prioritize risks related to equipment failures or disruptions in the supply chain, given their significant impact on production.

4. Develop Contingency Plans:
- Create specific, actionable plans for each identified risk. Clearly outline the steps to take, roles and responsibilities, communication protocols, and necessary resources.
- Example: A financial institution might develop a contingency plan for a data breach, including steps to isolate affected systems, notify customers, and work with cybersecurity experts to resolve the issue.

5. Resource Allocation:
- Allocate the necessary resources, including personnel, finances, and technology, to implement and execute the contingency plans effectively.
- Example: An IT company might allocate funds for cybersecurity tools, hire a response team, and invest in employee training to prevent and address potential cyber threats.

6. Communication Strategy:
- Establish a clear communication plan for internal and external stakeholders. Ensure that communication channels are identified, and key messages are prepared to minimize confusion during a crisis.
- Example: A hospitality business might have a communication plan in place to inform guests and staff about emergency evacuation procedures in the event of a natural disaster.

7. Training and Drills:
- Train employees on the contingency plans and conduct regular drills to ensure that everyone is familiar with their roles and responsibilities during a crisis.
- Example: A healthcare facility might conduct regular emergency response drills to prepare staff for situations like natural disasters or disease outbreaks.

8. Regular Review and Updating:

- Continuously review and update contingency plans to account for changes in the business environment, technology, or other factors. Ensure that plans remain relevant and effective over time.
- Example: A software development company might regularly review and update its contingency plans to address emerging cybersecurity threats and technology vulnerabilities.

9. Collaboration and Coordination:

- Foster collaboration with external partners, suppliers, and relevant authorities. Establish coordination mechanisms to ensure a unified response to shared risks.
- Example: An airline company might collaborate with airports, government agencies, and other airlines to develop a coordinated response plan for disruptions such as natural disasters or airspace closures.

10. Legal and Regulatory Compliance:

- Ensure that contingency plans align with legal and regulatory requirements in your industry. This includes data protection regulations, safety standards, and other relevant laws.
- Example: A financial institution's contingency plans should comply with regulations governing customer data protection and financial stability.

By following these steps and customizing them to the specific needs of your organization, you can create a robust contingency planning framework. This proactive approach helps organizations not only survive unexpected challenges but also maintain operational resilience and minimize the impact of disruptions.

Self-Care Planning

Self-care planning involves creating intentional and personalized strategies to prioritize and nurture one's physical, mental, and emotional wellness. It is a proactive approach to maintaining health and preventing burnout. Successful self-care planning involves identifying individual needs, setting realistic goals, and incorporating regular self-care practices into one's routine. Here's a guide on how to achieve effective self-care planning, along with examples:

Steps to Achieve Self-Care Planning:

1. Self-Assessment:
- Reflect on your physical, mental, and emotional wellness. Identify areas that require attention and improvement.
- Example: Recognize signs of stress, fatigue, or emotional exhaustion, and acknowledge the need for self-care in those areas.

2. Identify Personal Needs:
- Determine specific areas of your life that contribute to your wellness. This could include physical health, mental stimulation, emotional support, social connections, and leisure activities.
- Example: If physical health is a priority, identify activities like regular exercise, a balanced diet, and sufficient sleep as crucial components of your self-care plan.

3. Set Realistic Goals:

- Establish achievable and realistic goals for self-care. Consider both short-term and long-term objectives that align with your identified needs.
- Example: Instead of aiming to exercise every day, set a realistic goal of exercising for 30 minutes three times a week to start.

4. Create a Self-Care Plan:

- Develop a structured plan that outlines the specific self-care activities you will incorporate into your routine. This could include daily, weekly, and monthly practices.
- Example: Your self-care plan might include daily mindfulness exercises, weekly social activities, and monthly self-reflection sessions.

5. Prioritize Self-Care Activities:

- Identify which self-care activities are most essential and prioritize them based on your current needs and circumstances.
- Example: If work stress is high, prioritize activities that promote relaxation and stress reduction, such as meditation or a calming evening routine.

6. Incorporate Diverse Activities:

- Include a variety of self-care activities that address different aspects of wellness. This ensures a holistic approach to self-care.
- Example: Balance physical activities (exercise), mental activities (reading or learning something new), and emotional activities (connecting with loved ones) in your self-care plan.

7. Schedule Regular Check-Ins:

- Set aside time for regular self-assessments to evaluate the effectiveness of your self-care plan. Adjust goals and activities as needed.
- Example: Schedule a monthly reflection session to assess your wellness, celebrate achievements, and identify areas for improvement in your self-care routine.

8. Establish Boundaries:
- Clearly define and communicate boundaries to protect your time and energy. Learn to say no to activities that may compromise your wellness.
- Example: Set boundaries on work hours, commit to taking breaks, and avoid overcommitting to social or professional obligations.

9. Seek Support:
- Engage with friends, family, or professionals who can provide support and encouragement in your self-care journey.
- Example: Share your self-care goals with a close friend who can check in on your progress or join you in certain self-care activities.

10. Celebrate Successes:
- Acknowledge and celebrate achievements in your self-care journey. Recognize the positive impact on your wellness and overall quality of life.
- Example: Celebrate milestones such as consistently sticking to your exercise routine, achieving a work-life balance, or successfully managing stress.

11. Adapt to Changing Circumstances:
- Be flexible and willing to adjust your self-care plan based on changes in your life, priorities, or external circumstances.
- Example: If a new work project demands more time, adjust your self-care plan to accommodate the increased workload without neglecting essential self-care practices.

12. Regularly Review and Update:
- Periodically review your self-care plan to ensure it remains relevant. Update it based on evolving needs, goals, and experiences.
- Example: If you've developed new interests or found more effective self-care practices, incorporate them into your plan for continuous improvement.

Remember, self-care is a dynamic and individualized process. Successful self-care planning involves ongoing self-awareness, adaptability, and a commitment to making choices that promote overall wellness.

Chapter 5

Mindfulness and Stress Reduction

Productivity isn't just about doing more; it's about doing the right things with focus and intention. This chapter will discuss the importance of mindfulness in staying present and reducing stress. You'll learn techniques for staying calm and collected, even in the face of high-pressure situations.

Mindfulness, rooted in ancient Eastern philosophies, has become a powerful tool for cultivating a heightened awareness of the present moment. Derived from Buddhist traditions, mindfulness found its way into Western psychology in the 20th century, primarily through the work of pioneers like *Jon Kabat-Zinn*. Today, it is widely recognized as a transformative practice for managing stress and enhancing overall wellness.

The Link Between Mindfulness and Stress:

At its core, mindfulness is about being fully present, paying attention to thoughts and feelings without judgment. The practice encourages a non-reactive awareness that can be a game-changer in the face of stress. When we are mindful, we create a mental space to respond thoughtfully rather than react impulsively.

Practical Applications for Productivity:

1. Mindful Breathing:
- Work Scenario: Before diving into a hectic workday, take a few minutes to engage in mindful breathing. Focus on each breath, allowing your mind to settle. This practice can provide a calm foundation for the day ahead.

2. Mindful Work Breaks:
- Work Scenario: Instead of rushing through lunch or mindlessly scrolling through social media during breaks, use this time for mindful activities. Step outside, savour your meal, or practice a brief meditation to recharge your mental energy.

3. Mindful Listening:
- Work Scenario: In meetings or conversations, practice mindful listening. Fully engage with the speaker, putting aside internal chatter and judgments. This not only enhances communication but also fosters a positive and collaborative work environment.

4. Mindful Task Switching:
- Work Scenario: When transitioning between tasks, take a moment to pause and reset. Acknowledge the completion of one task before moving to the next. This prevents the carryover of stress from one activity to another.

5. Mindful Reflection:
- Personal Life Scenario: At the end of the day, set aside time for mindful reflection. Consider the positive aspects of your day, acknowledge challenges without dwelling on them, and express gratitude. This practice promotes a sense of fulfilment and balance.

6. Mindful Technology Use:
- Personal Life Scenario: In our tech-driven world, practice mindfulness in technology use. When checking emails or social media, do so with intention. Avoid mindless scrolling and be aware of the impact of screen time on your wellness.

The Mindful Journey to Increased Productivity:

Mindfulness and stress reduction are interconnected, and their benefits extend far beyond simply managing stress. By incorporating mindfulness into your daily routine, you cultivate a mindset that enhances productivity in both your professional and personal life.

When stress is managed through mindfulness, cognitive function improves. You become better equipped to make decisions, solve problems, and adapt to changes. The clarity gained from mindfulness allows you to prioritize tasks effectively, avoiding the pitfalls of burnout and overwhelm.

Moreover, the practice of mindfulness nurtures emotional intelligence. You develop a heightened awareness of your emotions and those of others, fostering better relationships in the workplace and at home. This emotional resilience translates into increased capacity to navigate challenges with grace and composure.

As you embark on this journey of mindfulness and stress reduction, remember that it's not about achieving perfection. It's about building a sustainable and adaptable practice that aligns with your unique needs and circumstances. In the chapters that follow, we will delve deeper into specific mindfulness techniques, providing you with a toolkit to integrate mindfulness seamlessly into your life. Embrace the journey and discover the transformative power of mindfulness in unlocking your true potential.

Step-by-Step Guide: Mindfulness Breathing Exercises

Mindfulness breathing exercises are a powerful way to bring awareness to the present moment, reduce stress, and enhance overall wellness. Here's a step-by-step guide on how to conduct mindfulness breathing exercises:

1. Find a Comfortable Position:
- Sit in a comfortable and relaxed position. You can sit on a chair with your feet flat on the ground or cross-legged on a cushion. Keep your back straight but not rigid, allowing for natural and easy breathing.

2. Close Your Eyes or Soften Your Gaze:
- Close your eyes to minimize external distractions. If closing your eyes is uncomfortable or not possible, simply soften your gaze and focus on a point in front of you.

3. Bring Attention to Your Breath:
- Begin by directing your attention to your breath. Notice the sensation of each inhale and exhale. Pay attention to the rise and fall of your chest or the feeling of your breath as it enters and leaves your nostrils.

4. Establish a Natural Breathing Rhythm:
- Allow your breath to follow its natural rhythm. There's no need to force or manipulate your breathing. Observe it as it is, paying attention to the ebb and flow of each breath.

5. Counting Breaths (Optional):

- If you find it helpful, you can incorporate counting to focus your mind. Inhale, then silently count "one" as you exhale. Inhale again, counting "two" on the exhale. Continue counting each breath, starting over when you reach a specific number, like five or ten.

6. Acknowledge and Release Distractions:

- As you practice, your mind may wander. It's normal. When distractions arise—whether they're thoughts, sounds, or sensations—acknowledge them without judgment. Gently guide your focus back to your breath.

7. Explore Different Breathing Techniques:

- Experiment with various breathing techniques to enhance mindfulness. For example:
- Deep Belly Breathing: Inhale deeply, allowing your belly to expand, and exhale completely, feeling your belly contract.
- Box Breathing: Inhale for a count of four, hold for four, exhale for four, and pause for four.
- 4-7-8 Breathing: Inhale for a count of four, hold for seven, exhale for eight.

8. Body Scan (Optional):

- Expand your awareness beyond your breath by incorporating a body scan. Start at your toes and gradually move your attention up through your body, noticing and releasing tension.

9. Set a Timer:

- To help structure your practice, set a timer for a chosen duration. This can be as short as five minutes or longer, depending on your preference and available time.

10. Gradual Closure:

- As the timer signals the end of your mindfulness session, gradually bring your awareness back to the present moment. Wiggle your fingers and toes, and when you're ready, open your eyes.

Tips:
- Consistency is Key: Regular practice enhances the effectiveness of mindfulness breathing exercises. Aim for daily sessions, even if they're brief.
- Be Patient: The mind may resist stillness initially. Be patient with yourself and acknowledge that mindfulness is a skill that develops over time.
- Adapt to Your Needs: Modify the practice to suit your preferences. You can practice mindfulness breathing while walking, lying down, or even during daily activities.

Remember: Mindfulness breathing exercises are about cultivating awareness, fostering a non-judgmental mindset, and embracing the present moment with openness and curiosity. Over time, these practices can contribute to increased calmness, improved focus, and a greater sense of wellness.

Chapter 6

Self-Care and Work-Life Balance

Maintaining productivity doesn't mean neglecting self-care and personal life. We'll explore strategies to achieve a healthy work-life balance, ensuring that you have time for relaxation, hobbies, and spending quality moments with loved ones.

The concepts of self-care and work-life balance have deep historical roots, with ancient philosophies emphasizing the importance of holistic wellness. However, it was in the latter half of the 20th century that these concepts gained prominence in response to the growing awareness of the impact of modern lifestyles on mental, emotional, and physical health.

Self-care is not a luxury; it is a necessity for maintaining a healthy and fulfilling life. At its core, self-care involves intentional actions to nurture your physical, emotional, and mental wellness. The practice empowers individuals to recharge, preventing burnout and fostering resilience in the face of life's demands.

Practical Strategies for Self-Care and Work-Life Balance:
1. Establish Boundaries:
   - Work Scenario: Clearly define work hours and stick to them. Communicate your boundaries to colleagues and avoid the temptation to check emails or complete tasks outside of designated work hours.

2. Prioritize and Delegate:

- Work Scenario: Identify tasks that align with your strengths and skills. Delegate responsibilities when possible, allowing you to focus on high-priority tasks that contribute to your professional growth and satisfaction.

3. Schedule Breaks:

- Work Scenario: Incorporate short breaks throughout the day. Whether it's a walk, a brief meditation, or a moment to stretch, these breaks can rejuvenate your mind and enhance overall productivity.

4. Disconnect from Technology:

- Personal Life Scenario: Designate specific times to disconnect from electronic devices. Create tech-free zones, especially during meals or quality time with family and friends, to foster genuine connections and relaxation.

5. Cultivate Hobbies and Interests:

- Personal Life Scenario: Set aside time for activities you love. Whether it's reading, gardening, or playing a musical instrument, engaging in hobbies provides a valuable escape from daily stressors.

6. Practice Mindfulness and Relaxation Techniques:

- Combined Scenario: Integrate mindfulness practices into both work and personal life. Techniques such as deep breathing, meditation, or progressive muscle relaxation can help manage stress and enhance focus.

7. Learn to Say No:

- Combined Scenario: Assess your commitments and be willing to decline additional responsibilities when your plate is full. Saying no is an essential skill in preserving your time and energy for meaningful pursuits.

8. Set Realistic Goals:

- Combined Scenario: Establish achievable goals in both your professional and personal life. Realism in goal setting prevents unnecessary stress and allows for a sense of accomplishment as you meet your objectives.

9. Build a Support System:

- Personal Life Scenario: Cultivate relationships with friends and family who provide emotional support. Share your thoughts and feelings with trusted individuals, creating a network of encouragement and understanding.

10. Regular Health Check-ins:

- Combined Scenario: Schedule regular health check-ups to monitor your physical wellness. Addressing health concerns proactively contributes to a stronger foundation for both work and personal life.

The Synergy of Self-Care and Productivity:

Contrary to the belief that self-care is a detractor from productivity, it is, in fact, the secret ingredient to sustained high performance. By embracing self-care and maintaining a healthy work-life balance, you fortify your physical and mental reserves, fostering increased focus, creativity, and resilience.

Think of self-care as an investment in your most valuable asset: yourself. When you prioritize your wellness, you cultivate the energy and enthusiasm needed to excel in both your professional and personal pursuits. As we navigate the strategies and practices in the chapters ahead, remember that the journey to optimal self-care and work-life balance is a personalized one. Discover what works best for you and witness the transformative power of a life in harmony.

Chapter 7

Staying Motivated and Overcoming Challenges

Every journey towards increased productivity has its ups and downs. In this chapter, we'll discuss strategies for staying motivated, overcoming procrastination, and dealing with setbacks.

The essence of motivation has been explored across various philosophical and psychological traditions throughout history. From Aristotle's concept of "entelechy" to modern theories of intrinsic and extrinsic motivation, understanding what drives human behaviour has been a perennial quest. In the contemporary world, motivation is recognized as a dynamic force that propels individuals to achieve goals and overcome obstacles.

Contemporary psychologists like *Abraham Maslow* and *B.F. Skinner* contributed to our understanding of motivation by highlighting the role of human needs and reinforcement. Maslow's hierarchy of needs emphasizes that motivation is intricately linked to fulfilling fundamental human needs, ranging from physiological necessities to self-actualization. Skinner's reinforcement theory underscores the impact of rewards and punishments in shaping behaviour.

Practical Strategies for Staying Motivated:
1. Clarify Your Why:
- Work Scenario: Before embarking on a project, clearly define your purpose. Understand why the task is important, how it

aligns with your values, and the impact it can have on your goals. This clarity serves as a potent motivator.

2. Set SMART Goals:

- Work Scenario: Establish Specific, Measurable, Achievable, Relevant, and Time-bound goals. Break down larger objectives into smaller, manageable tasks. The achievement of these milestones fuels motivation by providing a sense of progress.

3. Cultivate Intrinsic Motivation:

- Combined Scenario: Find joy and meaning in the process, not just the outcomes. When you derive satisfaction from the journey itself, motivation becomes intrinsic, leading to sustained commitment and enthusiasm.

4. Create a Positive Environment:

- Personal Life Scenario: Surround yourself with positivity. Whether it's your workspace, home, or social circles, a positive environment fosters a mindset conducive to motivation and resilience.

5. Embrace Failure as a Learning Opportunity:

- Combined Scenario: Shift your perspective on failure. Instead of viewing it as a setback, see it as a valuable learning experience. Analyse what went wrong, adjust your approach, and use setbacks as stepping stones to success.

6. Break Tasks into Manageable Steps:

- Work Scenario: Large projects can be overwhelming. Break them into smaller, manageable tasks. Completing each step provides a sense of accomplishment, boosting motivation for the next phase.

7. Visualize Success:

- Combined Scenario: Envision yourself achieving your goals. Visualization is a powerful motivational tool that helps reinforce your commitment and instils confidence in your ability to overcome challenges.

8. Develop a Growth Mindset:

- Combined Scenario: Adopt a growth mindset by embracing challenges and seeing effort as a path to mastery. This mindset fosters resilience, persistence, and a willingness to learn from setbacks.

9. Find Accountability Partners:
- Personal Life Scenario: Share your goals with a trusted friend or family member. Having someone to hold you accountable can provide the encouragement needed to stay motivated, especially when faced with challenges.

10. Celebrate Small Wins:
- Work Scenario: Acknowledge and celebrate your achievements, no matter how small. Recognizing progress, even in minor accomplishments, reinforces a positive feedback loop and keeps motivation high.

11. Take Breaks Strategically:
- Combined Scenario: Schedule breaks to prevent burnout. Short breaks throughout the day refresh your mind and prevent fatigue, helping you maintain motivation over the long term.

12. Stay Connected to Your Values:
- Personal Life Scenario: Regularly reflect on your values and align your goals with them. When your actions are in harmony with your core values, you draw upon a deep well of motivation that sustains you through challenges.

Overcoming Challenges:

1. Develop Resilience:
- Combined Scenario: Cultivate resilience to bounce back from setbacks. View challenges as opportunities for growth and develop the ability to adapt to changing circumstances.

2. Seek Support:
- Personal Life Scenario: Don't hesitate to seek support when facing challenges. Whether it's from friends, family, or colleagues, sharing your concerns and seeking advice can provide valuable perspectives.

3. Break Challenges into Smaller Tasks:
- Work Scenario: When confronted with a complex challenge, break it down into smaller, more manageable components.

Addressing each part individually makes the overall challenge less daunting.

4. Learn from Setbacks:

- Combined Scenario: Instead of dwelling on setbacks, use them as learning opportunities. Analyse what went wrong, identify areas for improvement, and apply these lessons to future endeavours.

5. Practice Mindfulness:

- Combined Scenario: Incorporate mindfulness into your routine. Mindful practices can help you stay focused, reduce stress, and maintain a calm, centred mindset when facing challenges.

6. Embrace Change as an Opportunity:

- Work Scenario: Change is inevitable. Rather than resisting it, view it as an opportunity for growth and innovation. Adaptability is a key factor in overcoming challenges.

7. Take Care of Your Wellness:

- Personal Life Scenario: Prioritize self-care to maintain physical and mental wellness. When you're in good health, you're better equipped to face challenges with resilience and a positive mindset.

In the intricate dance of motivation and overcoming challenges, the key lies in cultivating a mindset that sees each obstacle as a stepping stone toward personal and professional growth. As we delve into the subsequent chapters, remember that motivation is a dynamic force, fuelled by a combination of internal drive, supportive environments, and strategic approaches to navigating challenges. Embrace the journey, draw inspiration from your aspirations, and unlock the immense potential within.

Clarify Your 'Why'

Clarifying your "why" is crucial for maintaining motivation because it provides a clear sense of purpose and significance behind your actions and goals. Understanding the underlying reasons and motivations behind what you do serves as a powerful anchor that keeps you focused, resilient, and committed. Here are several reasons why clarifying your "why" is essential for staying motivated:

1. Meaning and Purpose:

- Connection to Values: Your "why" is often closely tied to your core values and beliefs. When your actions align with your values, there is a deeper sense of meaning and purpose, making the pursuit more fulfilling and sustainable.

2. Intrinsic Motivation:

- Internal Drive: Knowing your "why" fosters intrinsic motivation, which comes from within. Intrinsic motivation is more sustainable than external motivators because it taps into your genuine interests, passions, and personal values.

3. Resilience in the Face of Challenges:

- Overcoming Obstacles: Challenges and setbacks are inevitable. When you have a clear understanding of why your goals matter to you, you're better equipped to navigate difficulties. Your "why" becomes a source of resilience, helping you persevere through tough times.

4. Goal Clarity and Focus:
- Guiding North Star: Your "why" serves as a guiding North Star, keeping you focused on the bigger picture. It helps you prioritize tasks and make decisions that align with your overarching objectives, preventing distractions and maintaining clarity.

5. Increased Commitment:
- Personal Investment: When you have a compelling "why," you are more likely to invest time, effort, and energy into your pursuits. This increased commitment enhances the likelihood of goal attainment and sustained effort.

6. Alignment with Personal Values:
- Consistency and Authenticity: Knowing your "why" ensures that your actions are in alignment with your personal values. This consistency fosters authenticity, reinforcing a sense of self and reducing internal conflicts.

7. Boosted Enthusiasm:
- Positive Mindset: Understanding your "why" injects enthusiasm into your endeavours. It shifts your mindset from viewing tasks as mere obligations to embracing them as meaningful steps toward a larger purpose.

8. Inspiration for Others:
- Leadership and Influence: If you are working within a team or leading others, a clear "why" can be inspirational. Communicating your motivations can create a shared sense of purpose, fostering a more motivated and cohesive group.

9. Goal Re-evaluation and Adjustment:
- Adaptability: As circumstances change, your "why" allows you to reassess and adjust your goals while maintaining alignment with your core motivations. This adaptability ensures that your pursuits remain relevant and meaningful.

10. Enhanced Decision-Making:
- Guiding Principle: Your "why" becomes a guiding principle in decision-making. When faced with choices, you can evaluate which option best aligns with your overarching purpose, making decisions that contribute to your long-term satisfaction and success.

In essence, clarifying your "why" is about tapping into the intrinsic drivers that fuel your passion and commitment. It transforms motivation from a fleeting emotion to a resilient force that sustains you through challenges and propels you toward meaningful accomplishments. Taking the time to reflect on your "why" can be a transformative step in your personal and professional journey.

Cultivate Intrinsic Motivation

Cultivating intrinsic motivation is crucial when trying to stay motivated because it taps into personal satisfaction, genuine interest, and a sense of fulfilment from within. Unlike extrinsic motivation, which comes from external rewards or pressures, intrinsic motivation is driven by internal factors such as passion, curiosity, and a deep sense of purpose. Here's why cultivating intrinsic motivation is so important:

1. Sustainability:

- Intrinsic motivation tends to be more sustainable over the long term compared to extrinsic motivation. While external rewards may provide a temporary boost, they often lose their effectiveness over time. Intrinsic motivation, on the other hand, stems from personal enjoyment and a genuine desire to engage in the activity, making it more enduring.

2. Increased Resilience:

- Intrinsic motivation contributes to greater resilience in the face of challenges. When individuals are intrinsically motivated, setbacks are seen as opportunities for learning and growth rather than as failures. This resilience helps individuals bounce back from obstacles with renewed determination.

3. Autonomy and Control:

- Intrinsic motivation is closely tied to a sense of autonomy and control. When individuals feel that they have the freedom to make choices and decisions in alignment with their interests and values, they are more likely to stay motivated. Autonomy fosters a sense of ownership and personal responsibility.

4. Personal Satisfaction:

- Intrinsic motivation is inherently linked to personal satisfaction and a sense of accomplishment. The joy derived from engaging in activities for their own sake, rather than for external rewards, contributes to a positive emotional experience. This satisfaction becomes a powerful motivator in itself.

5. Enhanced Creativity and Innovation:

- Intrinsic motivation fosters creativity and innovation. When individuals are motivated by a genuine interest in what they are doing, they are more likely to explore new ideas, take risks, and think outside the box. This intrinsic curiosity fuels a continuous desire for improvement and innovation.

6. Improved Performance and Learning:

- Intrinsic motivation is associated with improved performance and enhanced learning outcomes. When individuals are motivated by a love for the task at hand, they are more likely to invest time and effort in mastering it, leading to better results and a deeper understanding.

7. Personal Development:

- Cultivating intrinsic motivation is closely tied to personal development. Individuals who are intrinsically motivated often seek opportunities for growth and self-improvement. This proactive approach to personal development contributes to a continuous cycle of learning and achievement.

8. Adaptability and Flexibility:

- Intrinsic motivation is adaptable and flexible. Individuals driven by internal factors are more likely to adapt to changing circumstances, explore new interests, and adjust their goals based on evolving priorities. This adaptability ensures that motivation remains relevant over time.

9. Positive Work Environment:

- In organizations, fostering intrinsic motivation contributes to a positive work environment. Employees who find intrinsic value in their work are more likely to be engaged, collaborative, and invested in the success of the team, creating a positive and productive workplace culture.

10. Alignment with Personal Values:

- Intrinsic motivation is closely aligned with personal values. When individuals engage in activities that resonate with their core values, there is a natural sense of purpose and alignment. This alignment reinforces motivation and contributes to a sense of fulfilment.

Cultivating intrinsic motivation involves connecting with personal passions, finding meaning in activities, and aligning with one's values. Whether in the workplace or personal life, recognizing and nurturing intrinsic motivation enhances overall wellness, satisfaction, and the ability to stay motivated in the face of challenges.

Visualize Success

The practice of visualizing success has roots in various psychological and philosophical traditions. While it has gained popularity in modern self-help and personal development literature, the concept can be traced back to ancient philosophical and contemplative practices. Here are some key influences on the origin of visualizing success:

1. Ancient Philosophical Traditions:

- Stoicism: Stoicism, an ancient Greek philosophy, emphasized the importance of cultivating a strong and resilient mindset in the face of challenges. Visualizing potential challenges and outcomes was a Stoic practice aimed at preparing individuals to respond effectively to various situations.
- Eastern Philosophies: Practices such as mindfulness and meditation, rooted in Eastern philosophies like Buddhism and Hinduism, often involve mental imagery and visualization. Visualization is used as a tool to cultivate focus, clarity, and a positive mental state.

2. Positive Psychology:

- In the 20th century, positive psychology emerged as a field of study that focuses on human strengths and wellness. Positive psychologists, such as *Martin Seligman*, explored the impact of positive thinking and optimism on overall life satisfaction. Visualization of positive outcomes became a key component in this field.

3. Sports Psychology:

- Athletes have long employed visualization as a technique to enhance performance. The renowned sports psychologist *Albert Bandura* introduced the concept of self-efficacy, emphasizing the role of one's belief in their ability to succeed. Visualization plays a crucial role in building self-efficacy by creating mental images of successful performances.

4. Neuroscience and Cognitive Psychology:

- Advances in neuroscience and cognitive psychology have provided insights into the brain's ability to form mental images and the impact of mental rehearsal on performance. The concept aligns with the idea of neural plasticity, where mental practice can contribute to the development of neural pathways associated with specific skills.

5. New Thought Movement:

- The New Thought movement, which emerged in the late 19th and early 20th centuries, emphasized the power of positive thinking and the law of attraction. Influential figures like *Napoleon Hill* and *Wallace D. Wattles* wrote about the importance of envisioning success and attracting positive outcomes through focused visualization.

6. Self-Help and Personal Development Literature:

- In the latter half of the 20th century and into the 21st century, self-help and personal development literature popularized the concept of visualizing success. Authors and motivational speakers, such as *Tony Robbins*, *Brian Tracy*, and *Louise Hay*, incorporated visualization techniques into their teachings to help individuals achieve their goals.

7. Cognitive-Behavioural Therapy (CBT):

- Cognitive-behavioural therapy, a widely used therapeutic approach, acknowledges the impact of thoughts on emotions and behaviours. Visualization is sometimes incorporated into CBT as a technique to challenge and modify negative thought patterns, replacing them with more positive and constructive images.

While the specific terminology and techniques associated with visualizing success may vary across these traditions, the underlying principle remains consistent: the mind's ability to create mental images can influence thoughts, emotions, and behaviours, ultimately impacting one's approach to challenges and goal attainment.

This practice is crucial when trying to stay motivated for several reasons:
1. Positive Reinforcement:
- Visualizing success provides positive reinforcement for your goals. When you vividly imagine yourself achieving success, your brain registers it as a positive experience. This reinforcement encourages a more optimistic and motivated mindset.

2. Clarifies Goals:
- Visualization helps clarify and define your goals. By picturing the desired outcome, you create a mental roadmap that guides your actions. This clarity reduces ambiguity and increases motivation by providing a clear target to strive for.

3. Enhances Focus:
- The act of visualizing success directs your focus toward the endpoint rather than dwelling on potential obstacles or challenges. This enhanced focus can help you stay motivated by preventing distractions and maintaining a positive orientation toward your goals.

4. Boosts Confidence:
- Visualization boosts confidence by creating a mental image of yourself succeeding. When you repeatedly visualize success, you begin to believe in your ability to achieve your goals. Confidence is a key driver of motivation, as it reduces self-doubt and fear of failure.

5. Stimulates Motivation Centres in the Brain:
- Visualization activates the same neural pathways in the brain that are activated when you actually perform the actions you are visualizing. This stimulation of motivation centres reinforces your commitment to achieving your goals.

6. Cultivates a Positive Mindset:

- Visualizing success contributes to cultivating a positive mindset. It helps shift your focus from potential setbacks to the positive aspects of achieving your goals. This positive mindset becomes a powerful motivator, influencing your attitudes and behaviours.

7. Creates a Sense of Ownership:

- Visualization creates a sense of ownership and personal connection to your goals. When you see yourself succeeding, you develop a stronger emotional attachment to the outcome. This emotional investment fuels motivation and dedication to your objectives.

8. Aids in Overcoming Obstacles:

- When faced with challenges or setbacks, the mental images of success you've cultivated through visualization can serve as a source of motivation. Remembering the positive images can help you persevere through difficulties and maintain momentum.

9. Improves Performance:

- Visualization has been linked to improved performance in various fields, from sports to business. Athletes, for example, use visualization to mentally rehearse successful performances. This mental rehearsal enhances skill development and performance, contributing to sustained motivation.

10. Encourages Goal Persistence:

- Visualization encourages goal persistence. When you have a clear image of success in your mind, you are more likely to persist in the face of challenges. The mental images act as a driving force, urging you to keep moving forward.

11. Inspires Action:

- Visualization inspires action by making success feel more attainable. When you can see yourself achieving your goals, it becomes a tangible reality in your mind. This perception of attainability motivates you to take concrete steps toward making it a reality.

12. Promotes a Positive Feedback Loop:
- Visualization contributes to a positive feedback loop. The more you visualize success and experience the positive emotions associated with it, the more motivated you become. This positive reinforcement creates a self-perpetuating cycle of motivation.

Incorporating visualization into your routine can be a potent tool for maintaining motivation, increasing confidence, and staying focused on your goals. It is a simple yet effective technique that aligns your thoughts with your aspirations, contributing to a more positive and motivated mindset.

Develop a Growth Mindset

Developing a growth mindset is crucial when trying to stay motivated because it shapes your beliefs about learning, intelligence, and personal development. A growth mindset is the belief that abilities and intelligence can be developed through dedication, hard work, and learning. This contrasts with a fixed mindset, which assumes that abilities are innate and unchangeable. Here's why cultivating a growth mindset is important for motivation:

1. Embracing Challenges:
- Importance: A growth mindset encourages individuals to see challenges as opportunities for growth rather than insurmountable obstacles.
- Motivational Impact: When faced with challenges, those with a growth mindset are more likely to persist and view setbacks as a natural part of the learning process.

2. Persistence in the Face of Setbacks:
- Importance: Individuals with a growth mindset are more likely to persevere in the face of setbacks and failures.
- Motivational Impact: Rather than being discouraged by failures, individuals with a growth mindset see them as temporary setbacks that provide valuable learning experiences.

3. Effort as the Path to Mastery:
- Importance: A growth mindset emphasizes that effort is a key factor in achieving mastery.

- Motivational Impact: When effort is seen as a pathway to improvement, individuals are motivated to invest time and energy into their pursuits, understanding that improvement comes with consistent effort.

4. Learning from Criticism:
- Importance: Individuals with a growth mindset view constructive criticism as a valuable source of feedback for improvement.
- Motivational Impact: Rather than feeling threatened by criticism, individuals are motivated to learn from feedback, adapt, and continually refine their skills and knowledge.

5. Inspiration from Others' Success:
- Importance: Those with a growth mindset find inspiration in the success of others, seeing it as evidence that abilities can be developed over time.
- Motivational Impact: Witnessing the success of others becomes a motivating factor, encouraging individuals to strive for their own growth and accomplishments.

6. Adaptability to Change:
- Importance: A growth mindset fosters adaptability and a willingness to embrace change.
- Motivational Impact: When confronted with change, individuals with a growth mindset see it as an opportunity for learning and improvement rather than a threat, promoting motivation to adapt and thrive.

How to Achieve a Growth Mindset:
1. Acknowledge and Challenge Fixed Mindset Thoughts:
- Pay attention to thoughts that imply abilities are fixed and challenge them. Replace statements like "I can't do this" with "I can't do this yet" to foster a growth-oriented mindset.

2. View Challenges as Opportunities:
- Embrace challenges as opportunities for learning and growth. Recognize that facing challenges head-on can lead to new skills and increased resilience.

3. Celebrate Effort, Not Just Results:
- Shift the focus from outcomes to effort. Celebrate the effort put into a task, recognizing that progress often comes from dedication and hard work.

4. Learn from Setbacks:
- Instead of viewing setbacks as failures, see them as opportunities to learn and improve. Analyse what went wrong, adjust your approach, and apply the lessons learned to future endeavours.

5. Seek Feedback and Criticism:
- Actively seek feedback from others and view constructive criticism as a valuable tool for improvement. Use feedback as a means to refine your skills and knowledge.

6. Cultivate a Love for Learning:
- Foster a genuine love for learning new things. Approach challenges with curiosity, and view each learning experience as a chance to expand your knowledge and abilities.

7. Surround Yourself with a Growth-Minded Environment:
- Engage with individuals who have a growth mindset. A supportive environment that encourages learning, resilience, and effort can reinforce and enhance your own growth mindset.

8. Set Learning Goals:
- Focus on learning goals rather than performance goals. Instead of aiming solely for outcomes, set goals that emphasize acquiring new skills, expanding knowledge, and embracing the learning process.

9. Understand the Power of "Yet":
- Integrate the word "yet" into your vocabulary. For example, if you catch yourself saying, "I don't know how to do this," add "yet" to acknowledge the potential for future growth and learning.

10. Reflect on Your Progress:
- Regularly reflect on your journey and acknowledge the progress you've made. Recognize that growth is an ongoing process and celebrate the small victories along the way.

By consciously cultivating a growth mindset, you can shift your perspective on learning and development. This shift not only enhances motivation but also creates a foundation for continuous improvement and resilience in the face of challenges.

Chapter 8

Fitness and Productivity

The relationship between fitness and productivity is a dynamic and interconnected one. Engaging in regular physical activity not only improves physical health but also has profound positive effects on mental wellness and cognitive function. The origins of recognizing this link can be traced to ancient philosophies and later findings in modern science. Let's explore how fitness contributes to overall wellness and productivity, along with practical steps for starting a fitness journey:

1. Ancient Philosophies and Holistic Wellness:

- Ancient civilizations, such as those in Greece and India, recognized the importance of a balanced and healthy lifestyle. Philosophers like *Hippocrates* emphasized the idea of "a sound mind in a sound body," acknowledging the holistic connection between physical health and mental wellness.

2. Scientific Understanding and Endorphins:

- In the late 20th century, scientific research began unravelling the neurobiological benefits of exercise. Physical activity triggers the release of endorphins, neurotransmitters that act as natural mood lifters. Endorphins contribute to stress reduction and the alleviation of symptoms associated with anxiety and depression.

3. Cognitive Function and Brain Health:

- Regular exercise has been linked to improved cognitive function and brain health. Physical activity increases blood flow to the brain, promotes the growth of new neurons, and enhances overall cognitive performance. It is associated with better memory, attention, and problem-solving skills.

4. Stress Reduction and Mental Clarity:

- Fitness serves as a powerful stress management tool. Engaging in physical activity reduces the levels of stress hormones like cortisol and promotes the release of neurotransmitters that contribute to a calm and focused mind. Stress reduction, in turn, enhances mental clarity and productivity.

5. Energy Levels and Productivity:

- Contrary to common belief, regular exercise increases energy levels rather than depleting them. By improving cardiovascular health and increasing the efficiency of oxygen utilization, fitness contributes to sustained energy throughout the day, enabling individuals to tackle tasks with vigour.

Starting Your Fitness Journey:

Embarking on a fitness journey is a personal and gradual process. Here are practical steps to initiate and sustain your fitness endeavours:

1. Define Your Goals:

- Clearly articulate your fitness goals. Whether it's improving cardiovascular health, building strength, or enhancing flexibility, having specific objectives provides direction and motivation.

2. Choose Activities You Enjoy:

- Opt for activities that bring you joy. Whether it's jogging, cycling, dancing, or practicing yoga, selecting enjoyable exercises increases the likelihood of long-term commitment.

3. Start Small and Gradual:

- Begin with manageable routines. Overwhelming yourself with intense workouts at the outset may lead to burnout. Start with short sessions and gradually increase intensity and duration.

4. Establish Consistency:

- Consistency is key to seeing results. Design a realistic and sustainable workout schedule that aligns with your lifestyle. Even brief, regular workouts yield significant benefits.

5. Mix Cardiovascular and Strength Training:

- Incorporate a combination of cardiovascular exercises and strength training. Cardio enhances heart health and endurance, while strength training builds muscle mass and contributes to overall physical resilience.

6. Prioritize Recovery:

- Allow time for recovery between workouts. Adequate rest is crucial for preventing injuries and ensuring that your body can adapt and grow stronger.

7. Make it Social:

- Invite friends or join fitness classes to make your journey more enjoyable and social. Having a workout buddy can provide motivation and accountability.

8. Track Progress:

- Keep a record of your workouts and celebrate milestones. Tracking progress not only reinforces motivation but also helps you adjust your fitness routine as needed.

9. Listen to Your Body:

- Pay attention to your body's signals. If you experience pain or fatigue, give yourself time to rest and recover. Balancing intensity with rest is crucial for long-term success.

10. Explore Mind-Body Practices:

- Consider incorporating mind-body practices like yoga or meditation into your routine. These practices not only enhance physical flexibility but also contribute to stress reduction and mental clarity.

In conclusion, the origins of recognizing the link between fitness and productivity date back to ancient wisdom, and modern science continues to affirm and deepen our understanding of this connection. By integrating fitness into your lifestyle and adopting a mindful approach to wellness, you can experience not only improved health but also heightened productivity and a more resilient and focused mind. Remember, the journey is unique to you—start small, stay consistent, and enjoy the transformative benefits of an active and healthy lifestyle.

It's tough not knowing where to begin, so here's two examples of a 4-week beginner's and intermediate fitness training programs that combines cardiovascular exercise and strength training. Adjust the intensity and duration based on your fitness level, and always consult with a healthcare professional before starting a new fitness program.

Beginner's Program:

Week 1-2: Establishing a Foundation

Day 1: Cardio
- 20 minutes of brisk walking or jogging
- 10 minutes of bodyweight exercises (squats, lunges, push-ups)

Day 2: Rest or Light Activity

Day 3: Strength Training
- Bodyweight squats: 3 sets of 12 reps
- Push-ups (knee push-ups if needed): 3 sets of 10 reps
- Plank: 3 sets, hold for 20-30 seconds

Day 4: Cardio
- 25 minutes of cycling or elliptical training

Day 5: Rest or Light Activity

Day 6: Cardio
- 20 minutes of brisk walking or jogging
- 10 minutes of bodyweight exercises (lunges, push-ups, jumping jacks)

Day 7: Rest

Week 3-4: Introducing Variety and Progression

Day 1: Cardio
- 25 minutes of jogging or cycling
- 15 minutes of bodyweight exercises (squats, lunges, push-ups)

Day 2: Rest or Light Activity

Day 3: Strength Training
- Dumbbell squats: 3 sets of 10 reps
- Dumbbell bench press (or push-ups): 3 sets of 10 reps
- Plank with leg lifts: 3 sets, hold for 20-30 seconds

Day 4: Cardio
- 30 minutes of cycling or elliptical training

Day 5: Rest or Light Activity

Day 6: Cardio
- 25 minutes of brisk walking or jogging
- 15 minutes of bodyweight exercises (lunges, push-ups, mountain climbers)

Day 7: Rest

Tips:
- Gradually increase the intensity as you progress.
- Include a warm-up before each workout (5-10 minutes of light cardio and dynamic stretches).
- Cool down with static stretches after each session.
- Stay hydrated and listen to your body. If something feels uncomfortable, modify or skip the exercise.
- Adjust the program based on your schedule and preferences.

This program assumes that you have a solid foundation in basic exercises. Always consult with a healthcare professional before starting a new fitness program.

Intermediate Program:

Week 1-2: Building on Basics

Day 1: Cardio & Strength
- 10 minutes warm-up (light cardio)
- 3 sets of 12 reps:
- Barbell squats
- Bench press
- Bent-over rows
- 20 minutes moderate-intensity cardio (running, cycling)

Day 2: Rest or Light Activity

Day 3: Cardio & Core
- 15 minutes warm-up (light cardio)
- 3 sets of 15 reps:
  - Deadlifts
  - Overhead press
  - Plank with alternating leg lifts
- 25 minutes high-intensity interval training (HIIT) cardio

Day 4: Rest or Light Activity

Day 5: Cardio & Strength
- 10 minutes warm-up (light cardio)
- 4 sets of 10 reps:
  - Front squats
  - Dumbbell chest flyes
  - Pull-ups or lat pulldowns
- 30 minutes moderate-intensity cardio (cycling, elliptical)

Day 6: Rest or Light Activity

Day 7: Active Recovery
- 30-40 minutes of light activity (walking, yoga, swimming)

Week 3-4: Increasing Intensity

Day 1: Cardio & Strength

- 15 minutes warm-up (light cardio)
- 4 sets of 8 reps:
  - Barbell lunges
  - Incline bench press
  - T-bar rows
- 25 minutes HIIT cardio

Day 2: Rest or Light Activity

Day 3: Cardio & Core

- 20 minutes warm-up (light cardio)
- 4 sets of 12 reps:
  - Romanian deadlifts
  - Seated dumbbell press
  - Russian twists
- 35 minutes moderate-intensity cardio (running, cycling)

Day 4: Rest or Light Activity

Day 5: Cardio & Strength

- 15 minutes warm-up (light cardio)
- 4 sets of 8 reps:
  - Goblet squats
  - Cable chest flyes
  - Chin-ups or pull-ups
- 30 minutes moderate-intensity cardio (cycling, elliptical)

Day 6: Rest or Light Activity

Day 7: Active Recovery

- 30-40 minutes of light activity (walking, yoga, swimming)

Tips:

- Increase weights gradually to challenge your muscles.
- Adjust the program based on your progress and preferences.
- Include flexibility and mobility exercises.
- Stay hydrated and prioritize recovery.
- Listen to your body and modify exercises as needed.

This program aims to provide a balanced combination of strength and cardiovascular training for intermediate fitness levels. Modify as necessary to suit your individual needs and goals.

Please remember to consult a doctor before beginning any workout plans, especially if you suffer from any injuries and/or illnesses.

Chapter 9

Building Healthy Habits

Productivity is not a one-time achievement but a way of life. We'll explore how to build and maintain healthy habits that support your overall wellness and mental health. Practical tips on creating routines and staying consistent will be provided.

Origins and Evolution:

The history of building healthy habits as a means to enhance productivity is deeply rooted in various philosophical, cultural, and scientific traditions. Over centuries, different societies and thinkers have recognized the connection between wellness, personal habits, and one's ability to lead a productive and fulfilling life. Here's a brief overview of the historical evolution of this concept:

1. Ancient Philosophical Traditions:
- Greek Philosophy: Ancient Greek philosophers, such as *Socrates* and *Aristotle*, emphasized the importance of balance and moderation in all aspects of life. They believed in cultivating virtues and habits that contribute to overall wellness, arguing that a harmonious life fosters productivity and intellectual growth.
- Eastern Philosophies: In Eastern philosophies like Ayurveda, traditional Chinese medicine, and Buddhism, the emphasis

on holistic wellness is central. These traditions recognize the interconnectedness of physical health, mental clarity, and spiritual balance, promoting habits that align with nature and promote overall productivity.

2. Medieval and Renaissance Periods:

- During the medieval and Renaissance periods, the idea of the "healthy mind in a healthy body" gained prominence. Scholars like the Roman poet *Juvenal* and later humanists like *Erasmus* emphasized the link between physical health and intellectual pursuits. The Renaissance saw a renewed interest in classical ideas, reinforcing the importance of balanced living.

3. Industrial Revolution and Work Habits:

- The Industrial Revolution brought about significant changes in work habits and lifestyles. As people transitioned from agrarian to industrial societies, the nature of work shifted. Thinkers like *Robert Owen* and later management theorists recognized the need for healthy work environments and advocated for humane working conditions to enhance productivity.

4. Early 20th Century and Scientific Advances:

- The early 20th century witnessed scientific advances that further underscored the importance of health habits. The work of psychologists like *William James* and early behaviourists laid the groundwork for understanding how habits are formed and how they influence daily life and productivity.
- The connection between physical health and mental wellness gained prominence, with advancements in medical science highlighting the role of nutrition, exercise, and sleep in maintaining overall health.

5. Mid-20th Century and Self-Help Movement:

- The mid-20th century saw the emergence of the self-help movement, which popularized the idea that individuals have agency in shaping their lives. Authors like *Dale Carnegie, Napoleon Hill,* and *Norman Vincent Peale* emphasized the power of positive thinking, goal setting, and cultivating healthy habits for personal success.

- The concept of "positive mental attitude" became a central theme, encouraging individuals to adopt habits that contribute to a positive mindset, resilience, and increased productivity.

6. Late 20th Century and Wellness Movement:

- The late 20th century witnessed a growing interest in the wellness movement, encompassing physical, mental, and emotional wellness. This era saw the mainstream adoption of practices like yoga, meditation, and a focus on preventive health measures.
- Corporate wellness programs began to recognize the impact of employee wellness on productivity, leading to initiatives that promote healthy habits within the workplace.

7. 21st Century and Technological Advances:

- The 21st century brought technological advances that influenced how individuals approach building healthy habits. Mobile apps, wearable devices, and online platforms emerged to help people track their habits, set goals, and receive personalized feedback.
- The integration of technology with wellness practices has made it easier for individuals to incorporate healthy habits into their daily lives, with a particular focus on optimizing productivity.

8. Scientific Research on Habits and Productivity:

- In recent decades, scientific research on habits, behaviour change, and productivity has expanded significantly. Researchers like *Charles Duhigg*, author of *"The Power of Habit,"* have delved into the neuroscience and psychology behind habit formation, offering insights into how habits shape our lives and impact productivity.
- Evidence-based approaches to habit formation, including concepts like cue-routine-reward loops, have become influential in guiding individuals toward building sustainable and productive habits.

The historical trajectory of building healthy habits reflects a continuous recognition of the interconnectedness between physical wellness, mental clarity, and productivity. From ancient philosophical traditions to modern scientific research, the evolution of this concept underscores the enduring importance of cultivating habits that contribute to a balanced and fulfilling life.

Understanding Healthy Habits:

Healthy habits are recurring behaviours that contribute positively to your physical, mental, and emotional wellness. They are the cornerstone of a balanced and fulfilling life, fostering resilience and productivity in both personal and professional spheres.

Practical Strategies for Building Healthy Habits:

1. Start Small and Gradual:

- Personal Life Scenario: Begin with small, manageable changes. For instance, if you aim to improve your fitness, start with a short daily walk. Gradually increase the duration and intensity as your habit takes root.

2. Create a Routine:

- Work Scenario: Establish a daily routine that includes dedicated time for tasks and breaks. Having a structured routine not only enhances productivity but also provides a framework for incorporating healthy habits seamlessly.

3. Set Clear and Achievable Goals:

- Combined Scenario: Define clear and realistic goals. Instead of a vague objective like "exercise more," specify a target, such as "exercise for 30 minutes three times a week." Clarity increases motivation and success.

4. Use Triggers:

- Personal Life Scenario: Associate your new habit with an existing routine or trigger. For instance, if you want to develop a reading habit, link it to your morning coffee or bedtime routine. The trigger helps establish a consistent habit loop.

5. Track Your Progress:

- Work Scenario: Keep a record of your accomplishments. Whether it's using a productivity app to track completed tasks or maintaining a journal, monitoring progress reinforces positive habits and provides motivation.

6. Incorporate Social Support:

- Combined Scenario: Share your goals with friends, family, or colleagues. Having a support system encourages accountability and provides encouragement when faced with challenges.

7. Practice Mindful Eating:

- Personal Life Scenario: Cultivate mindful eating habits. Pay attention to the sensory experience of each meal, savouring flavours, and textures. This practice not only contributes to health but also enhances overall wellness.

8. Prioritize Sleep:

- Combined Scenario: Make quality sleep a priority. Establish a consistent bedtime routine, create a comfortable sleep environment, and aim for the recommended seven to nine hours of sleep per night.

9. Integrate Movement into Daily Life:

- Work Scenario: Incorporate physical activity into your workday. Take short breaks to stretch, use a standing desk, or practice desk exercises. These micro-movements contribute to physical wellness and combat sedentary habits.

10. Practice Stress Management Techniques:

- Combined Scenario: Develop stress management habits, such as deep breathing, meditation, or mindfulness. These practices enhance resilience and contribute to a calm and focused mindset.

11. Hydrate Mindfully:

- Personal Life Scenario: Cultivate a habit of mindful hydration. Keep a water bottle within reach and take regular breaks to hydrate. Staying well-hydrated positively impacts both physical and cognitive performance.

12. Set Boundaries:

- Work Scenario: Establish clear boundaries between work and personal life. Define specific work hours, and when the workday concludes, disengage to prioritize personal time. Boundaries contribute to a healthier work-life balance.

The Impact on Productivity:

Building and maintaining healthy habits has a profound impact on productivity in both professional and personal domains. When individuals prioritize their wellness, they experience a range of benefits that directly contribute to heightened productivity:

1. Enhanced Energy Levels:
- Regular exercise, adequate sleep, and mindful eating contribute to increased energy levels. This heightened energy translates into improved focus and productivity throughout the day.

2. Improved Cognitive Function:
- Healthy habits positively impact cognitive function. Adequate sleep, proper hydration, and regular physical activity are linked to enhanced memory, concentration, and problem-solving skills.

3. Reduced Stress and Burnout:
- Stress management practices and the establishment of work-life boundaries contribute to reduced stress levels. Lower stress enhances mental clarity, decision-making, and overall resilience against burnout.

4. Increased Resilience:
- The development of healthy habits fosters emotional and mental resilience. Individuals are better equipped to navigate challenges, setbacks, and uncertainties, maintaining a positive and proactive mindset.

5. Positive Work Environment:
- A workplace that encourages and supports healthy habits contributes to a positive work environment. Collective wellness enhances collaboration, morale, and a shared commitment to productivity.

6. Balanced Work-Life Integration:
- Prioritizing personal wellness through healthy habits contributes to a balanced work-life integration. This balance prevents burnout, promotes satisfaction, and creates a sustainable approach to productivity.

Cultivating a Lifestyle of Wellness:

Building healthy habits is not a short-term endeavour but a lifelong commitment to wellness. By integrating these practices into both work and personal life, individuals create a foundation for sustained productivity, resilience, and fulfilment. As you embark on this journey, remember that each small step contributes to a healthier, more vibrant life—one habit at a time.

The End, or Just The Beginning?

Final Thoughts

As we draw the final pages of *"Productivity and Wellness: The Key to A Brighter Future"* to a close, we embark on an ending that is, in reality, a new beginning. This journey of exploration, insight, and transformation has taken us through the intricate web of productivity and its profound connection to our mental health and overall wellness. We've uncovered the science behind the link between productivity and mental health, revealing the ways in which our actions and choices can reduce stress and anxiety while elevating self-esteem and happiness. We've witnessed the transformative power of setting and achieving goals, mastering time management, and embracing mindfulness in our daily lives.

The essence of productivity, as we've discovered, isn't about squeezing more into your day but about maximizing the quality of your existence. It's about finding your true purpose, achieving your goals, and connecting with your inner self. It's about balancing the demands of a fast-paced world with the need for self-care and meaningful human connections. Through the inspiring stories of those who have walked this path before us, we've learned that productivity isn't a one-size-fits-all formula. It's a personalized journey of self-discovery and continuous improvement. As you close this book, I encourage you to remember that productivity is not a destination; it's a way of life. It's a lifelong commitment to taking charge of your time and energy to create a life that aligns with your values and aspirations.

As you venture forth, remember that the pursuit of productivity and wellness is not without its challenges. There will be setbacks, moments of doubt, and times when the juggling act becomes overwhelming. But just as we've learned throughout this book, these challenges can be overcome. Your resilience and determination can carry you through even the toughest of times. The pages of this book are now but stepping stones on your journey towards a more productive, balanced, and fulfilling life. It is my hope that you'll carry the wisdom, strategies, and inspiration found here with you as you navigate the ever-changing landscape of your life.

Ultimately, productivity is your path to mental health and happiness. It's the key to unlocking your full potential and living a life of purpose and contentment. The journey is yours to embark upon, and the possibilities are boundless.

"Thank you for joining me on this voyage of self-discovery and personal growth. Your life has the potential to be as extraordinary as you choose to make it. So, with newfound insights and renewed determination, embrace the path to productivity, and in doing so, embrace a future filled with wellness, resilience, and the contentment that you truly deserve."

Richard Sharratt

Unleash Your Full Potential, One Task At A Time!

Have you ever wished to become the best version of yourself. Join our community and upgrade your skills, energize your body, and nurture your mind – all in one place.

NO monthly subscriptions.
FREE monthly content updates.

Are you ready to <u>unleash</u> your full potential?

Download *ProductivityGo* TODAY and embark on a holistic journey towards success and wellness!

In the App Stores for both Android and IOS in early 2024.

ProductivityGo

References

Shian-Ling, Keng. '*Clinical Psychology Review*'. Department of Psychology and Neuroscience, Duke University, Durham, NC 27708, United States, 2011. Effects of mindfulness on psychological health: A review of empirical studies - ScienceDirect

Suzanne Segerstrom, PhD, MPH. '*Psychosomatic Medicine*', 2023, Psychosomatic Medicine (lww.com)

Vermote, Branko. Morbee, Sofie. Soenens, Bart. Vansteenkiste, Maarten. Waterschoot, Joachim. Beyers, Wim. Van Der Kapp-Deeder, Jolene. '*How Do Late Adults Experience Meaning During the COVID-19 Lockdown? The Role of Intrinsic Goals*', Journal of Happiness Studies, 2023, How Do Late Adults Experience Meaning During the COVID-19 Lockdown? The Role of Intrinsic Goals | Journal of Happiness Studies (springer.com)

Wright, Rebecca. '*Shared motivations in Dopamine*', Nature Reviews Neuroscience, 2023, Shared motivations in dopamine | Nature Neuroscience

Colin Wayne Leach and Richard E. Lucas. '*Journal of Personality and Social Psychology*', 2023, Journal of Personality and Social Psychology (apa.org)

Valcour, M. '*Work-based resources as moderators of the relationship between work hours and satisfaction with work-family balance*'. Journal of Applied Psychology, 92(6), 2007, Work-based resources as moderators of the relationship between work hours and satisfaction with work-family balance. (apa.org)

Wang, Ping. Wang, Xiaochun. '*Effects of Time Management training on Anxiety, Depression and Sleep Quality*', National Institute of Health, 2018, Effect of Time Management Training on Anxiety, Depression, and Sleep Quality - PMC (nih.gov)

Svartdal, Frode. Granmo, Sjur. Faerevaag, Fredrik. 'On the behavioural side of procrastination: Exploring behavioural delay in real-life settings', National Library of Medicine, 2018, On the Behavioral Side of Procrastination: Exploring Behavioral Delay in Real-Life Settings - PMC (nih.gov)

Russo, Marcello. Shteigman, Anat. Carmeli, Abraham (2016) 'Workplace and family support and work–life balance: Implications for individual psychological availability and energy at work', The Journal of Positive Psychology, Journal of Personality and Social Psychology, 2018, Workplace and family support and work–life balance: Implications for individual psychological availability and energy at work: The Journal of Positive Psychology: Vol 11, No 2 (tandfonline.com)

Trautwein, Ulrich. Lüdtke, Oliver. Köller, Olaf. Baumert, Jürgen. 'Self-esteem, academic self-concept, and achievement: How the learning environment moderates the dynamics of self-concept', American Psychology Association, 2006, Self-esteem, academic self-concept, and achievement: How the learning environment moderates the dynamics of self-concept. (apa.org)

Menardo, Elisa. Di Marco, Donatella. Ramos, Sara. Brondino, Margherita. Arenas, Alicia. Costa, Patricia. Vaz de Carvalho, Carlos. Pasini, Margherita. 'Nature and Mindfulness to Cope with Work-Related Stress: A Narrative Review', International Journal of Environmental Research and Public Health, 2022, IJERPH | Free Full-Text | Nature and Mindfulness to Cope with Work-Related Stress: A Narrative Review (mdpi.com)

Bailey, Ryan. 'Goal setting and action planning for Health Behaviour Change', American Journal of Lifestyle Medicine, 2017, Goal Setting and Action Planning for Health Behavior Change - PMC (nih.gov)

Matthews, Gail (Dr). 'Goal Research Summary', Dominican University of California, 2023, gailmatthews-harvard-goals-researchsummary.pdf (dominican.edu)